JOURNAL

of a

COLLECTOR

—

I gave up my
life for you.

JOURNAL

of a

COLLECTOR

—

ALISTAIR McALPINE

Illustrations by John Glashan

DEDICATION
To Romilly, my wife and travelling companion, with love.

With many thanks to Min Hogg, Editor of *The World of Interiors*,
and Stephen Fay, formerly Editor of *Business Magazine*, for all their
tolerance and encouragement.

First published in Great Britain in 1994 by
PAVILION BOOKS LIMITED
26 Upper Ground, London SE1 9PD

Text copyright © Alistair McAlpine 1994
Illustrations copyright © John Glashan 1994

Designed by Nigel Partridge

A CIP catalogue record for this book is available from the British Library.

ISBN 1 85793 433 4

Typeset in Ehrhardt 10½/12½ pt

Printed and bound in Great Britain by Butler and Tanner Ltd,
Frome and London

2 4 6 8 10 9 7 5 3 1

This book may be ordered by post direct from the publisher. Please
contact the Marketing Department. But try your bookshop first.

Contents

INTRODUCTION

NEAR the edge of Plympton, a small town in Devon, stood a row of Victorian cottages. That was in the late 1950s, when I last visited Plympton. Perhaps Plympton is a large town now and these cottages have been torn down to make way for a concrete town hall or some other municipal building. I do not know, and it does not matter a lot, for the most interesting features of these buildings were their inhabitants. The Andrade family has, I am certain, long since died. I arrived at their home one day just before lunch. I was shown into their kitchen and offered refreshments. I cannot recall what the younger member of that family, or indeed his wife, looked like, but I do recall their old uncle, who sat wrapped in a rug. I was introduced to him as a young man interested in arms and armour; he to me as a great scholar on the subject of armour. The Andrades were general dealers in the old sense, and supplied from their row of cottages called Borgian Villas most of the antique trade in the west of England. These cottages were filled with every conceivable type of antique and there was one room that I remember as if I stood there today, a room filled with Staffordshire pottery. Most of it dated from the mid-19th century, and there was in this room a large quantity of dross, but among it great rarities. You purchased the first pieces that came to hand (you could not choose only the good, or reject the bad). There was no other way, as the pottery was packed so tightly that only the pieces at the front were accessible. There was no place to stand the pieces that you pulled out – in order to be able to compare them, one with the other, you bought the pottery as it came, or not at all.

My life has been a little like that room. I have had a mass of experiences, some pleasant, some sad, many downright inconvenient at the time. In the spring of 1987 I began to write of them, and slowly one memory jogged another, pieces from my past were uncovered, like the pottery from the Andrades' cottage. Some were only fragments, some complete; some commonplace, some rare – to me at least. So this book began. I had intended to start this introduction with the words 'I am a collector'. Then, as I thought about that statement, I realized quite how misleading it would be. True, I have collected items as diverse as snowdrops and chickens, police truncheons and paintings by the American abstract impressionists. I collect, I suppose, to learn; for I have never collected to possess. When a collection passes from my hands it goes in total – nothing remains, no momento. No object or painting has such beauty that I could not bear to part with it. Wander around my home and you will find little evidence of past enthusiasms. My true collection is in my mind, helped by a notebook, phrases that people have spoken to me, a description of a room, a meal, a rare plant, a journey, the tales of travellers and travel. Slowly, over many years, this collection has accumulated.

It began in early childhood, for my mother was strongly of the view that the only proper form of education was that gained by travel. We travelled extensively, mostly by boat, in the last days of the great ocean liners, or by train – when railway trains offered a real service and air travel was still a primitive affair. I recall the amazement of my family (we always travelled as a family) when the steward on board a Viscount belonging to British European Airways explained to us that the plane was so stable that you could stand a half-crown on its edge – minutes later the aircraft hit an air-pocket and coffee cups were thrown up to the ceiling and showered down their contents on all the passengers. I loved the railway stations and docks, the bustle and departure – it is in my blood, and I have no doubt that that desire to travel accounted for my wanderings in Britain searching for a particular painting or book. Barely a weekend passed that I did not scour the flea-markets or travel to discover what goods the country dealers had bought that week. In the same way that I sat in the Andrades' kitchen and listened to their old uncle as he spoke about armour, over the years so I have listened to the tales of a thousand dealers – from Bond Street to Perth in Western Australia. And now these memories have become my stock in trade.

ONE

COLLECTOR'S ITEMS

BEWARE OF THE SQUIRRELS

DEALERS buy and sell. That is their temperament; they were not born to collect. The best dealers take nothing home to keep for themselves. Some of the worst dealers, on the other hand, respond to a show of enthusiasm at a piece in their shop with a sniff: 'This is so beautiful, I'm keeping it for myself. Not for sale.' (This remark

you're too
perfect
to sell

is often accompanied by a quite grand manner.) This may be a sales tactic of course, but more often it is downright stupidity, so unprofessional that if he were a member of that even older profession, this dealer would incite his clients to violence. In any event, this attitude irritates me beyond endurance. Museums are for looking at masterpieces, and shops are for buying them in.

As with all inflexible rules, there is the odd exception. The fact is that some capable dealers do take fine items home so they can take them back to the shop when business is slack and in need of the encouragement of an exciting 'new' piece. I recall a story that makes this point, about one of the world's great dealers, who has officially retired, which means that he sees only the customers he is inclined to see, and buys only occasionally when he sees something he is inclined to buy.

This great man was approached by a friend of mine – a dealer, who was still involved in the hurly-burly of the antique trade, listening to what the runners had to offer and trading with our dealers; all were involved in the excitment of the hunt for new stock. About half a dozen times a year my friend took time off to visit the great man to talk and buy a few objects.

For many years he admired a carved agate head. It was the head of a caesar from imperial Rome, a few inches high. For years this head had been beyond my friend's means, but as the volume of his business grew, so did the profits. Naturally, the price of the agate head grew, too, but recently, after much heart-searching – and indeed after some pocket-searching – my friend broached the subject: 'That agate head,' he said, 'the one you have had for years. How much is it?'

'I have had that head for the best part of 30 years. Nobody wanted it much and I was glad to keep it. Not for sale,' the old man replied.

'How much is it now? It would be for myself.'

The old dealer held the head in his palm and said: 'One day it will be yours, but not now. For the moment I still need this piece.' Both men appear to have broken cardinal rules of ethical dealing: the older man showed a piece that was not for sale, and the younger man tried to buy it for himself. I have to confess that I have only praise for them and I must explain why, for the moral is that even the most inflexible rules are sometimes subordinate to manners.

Had I seen the agate head of a Roman caesar in a shop and, having asked the price, been informed somewhat charmlessly by the dealer that although I was correct to have identified the piece as a good one, it was not for sale, this would have been an inexcusable breach of the rules. Since, however, the exchange between the old dealer and my friend was conducted with discretion and style and contained the promise of eventual satisfaction, the breach of the rules was entirely acceptable.

This leads me to my second proposition: while dealers ought to stick to the rules, the buyer – our collector – may do entirely as he or she pleases. In the early 1970s, I had a bookshop. I dealt in a great variety of books, hand-coloured folios, the great flower and bird books, French editions bound by famous binders and illustrated by great painters. I sold fat volumes of autobiography and slim volumes of verse.

One of my clients was a painter: he was famous and rich and he loved to buy. I think he loved to buy more than he loved to paint. He was a wonderful client.

After a few years in the book trade I moved my house to the country and closed the business. I put my stock under the hammer and thought no more about book-selling. Some time later I visited the famous painter. He showed me his studio and his very beautiful house. The quality was no surprise because I knew from the books that he had bought from me that his taste was impeccable, for his taste ran from Redouté to Cubist Picasso.

The books were worth a fortune, and when he showed me the room in which he kept them, they were all still there. Indeed, they were intact in the literal sense that they were still in the wrappings in which they had left my shop. There is in all of us a squirrel instinct – the desire to buy and put away – and my painter friend has succumbed to it totally, but since the role of the collector is to collect, there is nothing wrong with squirrelling at all. Only among dealers does it become unforgiveable, for among them it amounts to little less than restraint of trade.

Beyond the Repair

SADLY, some antique dealers allow themselves to be carried away by the enthusiasm of a prospective client who wants to believe that a piece is better than it is. In such circumstances the dealer sometimes omits a full description of the restoration that was necessary to make the piece look as it does.

The morality is clear. It should be assumed that restoration has been carried out on all antiques that are not declared perfect. In the case of pictures, furniture and antiquities some restoration is acceptable. What matters, and affects the price, is the degree. What appears to be a bargain might turn out to have been very expensive if an infra-red examination reveals more restoration than has been confessed to.

This is where the debate becomes more complex. Few collectors have access to an infra-red light, so they discover how much restoration has been done only when they try to sell. To avoid this predicament, my advice is steadfast: always buy from reputable dealers and buy top-class goods. With china or glass, buy nothing that has been repaired. Most of all, ask about the condition of a piece and ask clearly; misunderstandings can occur even in the best-ordered establishments.

Which reminds me of a story of the Lady of Title – as they call them in the catalogues produced by better salerooms – who was intent on making a sizeable purchase on Bond Street. Uncertain of the exact location of the shop she sought, she went into an antique dealers and asked: 'Could you direct me to Hook Nose, the bookmaker, I forgot whether he is up the street or down it.'

'Just one moment,' the dealer replied and went into a huddle with his colleagues at the back of the shop. As they had never heard of the establishment, they summoned a member of staff who followed the horses.

'Never heard of him, guv'ner,' he answered.

'Foolish boy,' exclaimed one of the partners. 'You must have. Hook Nose. A nickname, obviously.'

But the boy insisted, so the partner returned to the counter. 'Excuse me, my lady,' he asked, 'but is this Hook Nose by chance known by any other name?'

'Hook Nose?' she repeated, sounding like Lady Bracknell.

'The bookmaker, my lady.'

'Bookmaker?' she bellowed. 'I was enquiring about Hoot and Knowles, the bookmakers.'

The moral of this story is that if you want to know the right answer, ask the right person the right questions. If you want to know about silver, consult the proprietors of S.J. Phillips, and if you want to know the way, ask a policeman.

There is, of course, more to restoration than meets the eye. I am reminded of a friend who moved in next door to a keeper of rabbits. Her neighbour warned that if her two small dogs troubled his rabbits they would be destined for the Great Kennel in the Sky. Having promised to control the dogs, you can imagine my friend's distress when they frisked into the house carrying a dishevelled dead rabbit. Frantic, she undertook some refurbishment herself, washing the corpse and blow-drying the fur with her own hairdrier, before sneaking over the garden fence and returning the restored rabbit to its hutch.

Some days later while out walking the dogs, she met the rabbit's owner. Noticing that he looked pale and seemed distracted, she asked him: 'Rabbits all right?'

'Not really,' he answered. 'I'm worried, worried sick. Just last week one of my rabbits died and I buried it, and two days later it was back in the hutch, still dead, but looking better than new.'

I am afraid I have encountered dealers who have had a similar experience with their stock. It had been radically restored, they confessed, but it was like a miracle, for they had no idea how.

The very best antique dealers would not allow for any misinterpretation or ambiguity, as can be judged from the experience of the Fabius family in 1968. Fabius père owns a fine shop near the rue Faubourg St Honoré in Paris, and is celebrated for his insistence that words and descriptions should mean what they say. Fabius fils was a clever young man – he later became a socialist prime minister of France – but in 1968 he was a revolutionary. Returning home one night, tired but happy after a good day's rioting, he told his father that he had burned the fine cars of 25 capitalist pigs.

'Papa,' he said, 'you have no idea of the joys of the revolution.'

'My son,' Fabius père replied, 'I understand exactly, for this very day I, too, have set fire to a car.'

'Bravo,' the boy cried, 'where did this happen?'

The father took his son to the window and pointed to the burned-out red Porsche in the street below.

It was his son's own car.

This dealer I would trust, happily, any day.

THE BURGLING CLASSES

THE moral of these cautionary tales is that things are not always what they seem and the first is the story of an antique dealer. He was a real expert – by which I mean a man who has spent his life looking at silver. (A few of us believe that he may have spent a number of previous incarnations dealing in silver as well.)

A few years ago this expert's house was burgled. This experience is devastating when all the thieves take is your television set. In this case they had rather better taste and careful fingers, for they stole with discernment and care his whole collection, including a Chinese porcelain bowl of the 17th century mounted in silver.

This blow caused him great distress, not so much because of the value of these items, but because they were the encrustations of a career in antique dealing. Some years later he recovered in part from this setback when he was walking in a fashionable street in Paris. As in the habit of a lifetime, he turned his eyes to the window of any antique shop he passed. In one he saw a 17th-century Chinese porcelain bowl, mounted in silver, similar to the one that had been stolen from him.

Entering the shop, he bargained for an hour, bought the bowl, and with great delight, returned to London. He told his sons it was a fine bowl; though it was larger than the one he had lost – similar, but larger. Similar, much better quality, and – hard though it was to believe it – only half the cost of his original highly treasured bowl.

A year or two passed and, as sometimes happens; the thieves were caught and the dealer's possessions were returned to him – with the exception of the Chinese bowl. Strange as this rare coincidence may seem, that bowl had been sold by the thieves and ended up in a Paris antique shop. He had, without knowing it, bought his own bowl back, which proves that, because not everything is what it seems, some objects that are different can, in fact, be the same.

Incidentally, although I have been burgled three or four times, the thieves have always treated my collection with contempt. Maybe it was the thought of putting 900 policemen's truncheons in the swag bag. Perhaps it was more subtle: that truncheons formerly used by policemen put off these thieves in the same way that the impedimenta of the Aboriginal witch doctor worries me. Although they are of incredible beauty, I won't have them in the house.

On another occasion the foolish thieves bypassed a 20-foot Mark Rothko, a fine modern American painter. I suspect that the burgling classes are probably against abstract art; at least, when it is on that scale. But I am bound to confess, however, that they were not taken by my collection of American rag dolls (or, rather, that they did not take any).

(Another time when I was burgled, the thieves even passed up my television set. Although it was not the latest model, the burglars regarded it as they had my collections – with contempt.)

Maybe I am lucky, but whatever the reason, it is a fact that as burgled objects move from hand to hand, they do sometimes, by chance break. So, in this curious world of collecting, there is a strata of antiques, broken antiques, with dealers and collectors who like broken objects.

This is an area of colossal profit for a dealer who has a good restorer in tow – an area heavily populated for instance, by the interior decorators who furnish whole buildings like those new London 'clubs'; an area where the commonplace becomes the fantastic; where the colour of a settee can be adjusted to matching the curtains; where the bottom of one piece or the top of another become little masterpieces in their own right, and since everything is not what it seems, an Italian confessional can be transformed into a bookcase.

However, one dealer with a shop in a small Sussex town had no such intention. He bought broken pieces to fill his window. Every piece had a serious defect. But there was no desire to deceive the unwary (and, to be quite honest, you would have to be very unwary to be deceived by his stock). The dealer used the shop to show that he was in the market: he wanted to buy not sell.

He was very pleased with his shop, which was situated at the bottom of a long hill. One day the dealer was out of the shop buying somewhere, which was fortunate because a large lorry carrying something heavy like bricks ran out of control down the hill straight through the shop. You can imagine the mess. The shop was demolished and the stock, which was already in pieces, was in even more pieces. However, only the dealer knew that and, on his return, he was seized not with sadness, but with joy. The Brittle clause and, for that matter, every other clause in his insurance policy, was activated by the crash. At his feet lay his fortune.

My desire, however, is to tell cautionary tales. So I want to tell you that when you see a wardrobe just like the one in your great aunt's backroom fetch a prodigious price in Christie's, do not assume they are the same. Do not waste hours charming your great aunt, then attaching this heavy piece of furniture to the top of your motor car, and leaving it standing in the foyer of the auctioneer's King Street premises. The likelihood is that there will be a subtle difference, like 100 years or so in its age.

You cannot imagine how extremely unattractive a large wardrobe can be in these circumstances. Not even the burglars want it. They will leave you with the wardrobe, if with nothing else. The best you could hope for is that, as it stands on the kerb waiting to be taken to your home, it might be run over by a bus. As with politicians, this does not happen often.

Dragons' Eggs at a Price

WE all make mistakes. The greatest expert will sometimes identify the genuine article as a fake. The greatest novice can buy a masterpiece in the street market for a few pounds, aquiring a fortune and a reputation simultaneously. The novice feels no embarrassment; the expert can cover his chagrin with the mystery and cloaks of expertise.

I have a friend in a nearby town – a dealer in antiques – who needed to invoke more than mystery to cover his embarrassment over the matter of a fine pair of 17th-century brass chandeliers. A dealer who was known to him, but for whom he harboured a deep suspicion, arrived at his shop in the main street. 'Come and look,' he said, taking my friend out to the back of his van. My friend looked at the chandeliers and immediately asked: 'How much?'

'I think I'll take them to London; they're probably a bit rich for you,' replied the dealer.

'Come on, quote a price,' said my friend, a little sharply.

'Five thousand pounds.'

'Done.'

One chandelier was hung in each of his two windows, and as soon as they were up, a caller commented: 'My God, these are good.' He spoke truer than he knew.

He was followed into the shop by two more callers: a policeman and a parson.

The conversation lacked the usual polite preliminaries. Instead the policeman said: 'What are you doing with stolen goods in your shop?'

My friend, who was not only innocent but nonplussed, bridled. The parson then chimed in: 'These chandeliers are from my church.'

'Rubbish, I bought them only this morning from a dealer. I have the receipt right here.'

'This morning you may have bought them, but last night they hung in my church,' said the parson.

Though his posture was becoming increasingly defensive, my friend refused to submit until the policeman said: 'Those chandeliers have hung for 300 years in a church a few yards from your shop and you have the nerve to tell us that you have never seen them.'

Desperate, my friend said: 'I have never been inside the church. I am Jewish.'

The policeman and the parson left, taking with them £5,000 worth of chandeliers. My friend, who was not merely embarrassed, but very cross, set out to recover his money. This proved much more difficult than spending it.

This embarrassment was as nothing compared to the mortification experienced by the uncle of a famous West End picture dealer. Seeking to do his nephew a good turn, he wrote to Mr Mellon, a prince among American collectors, who was visiting London at the time, telling him of a particularly fine Turner he had seen by chance hanging in a West End Gallery. His nephew recommended the Turner most highly; he said the price was cheap – well, very reasonable – and that it was a snip that Mr Mellon should not resist.

He then wrote a second letter to his nephew, explaining what he had done, adding that Mr Mellon was a man with plenty of cash – really, plenty – and that he should push up the price because Mr Mellon was capable of paying big money for a Turner. The letters were posted and duly arrived. When they were opened, however, the West End dealer read a letter written to Mr Mellon. It was clear that Mr Mellon would be reading a fond letter from an uncle to his nephew.

Mr Mellon, a man of style, guessed what had happened and drove directly to the shop and acquired the Turner for a price that was, for a Mellon, quite modest.

When the dealer saw his uncle, he said how curious it was to receive a letter recommending a Turner in his own shop from his own uncle. His uncle decided that the best way to deal with this discomfiture was a sudden attack of discretion.

Of course, some people are simply not susceptible to embarrassment. I recall two sculptor friends – one a Scotsman, the other a lady from Singapore, who had a son. He was a good-looking mixture of Scots and Chinese, and at the local school he soon exhibited the longing to trade that is the characteristic of both his antecedents. Unfortunately, he had no capital with which to buy the goods to sell. He was not, however, deterred. He summoned up the mystery of the Orient and it provided him with the solution. He decided to sell dragon's eggs. In his parents' garden he found a presentable collection of smooth stones; he priced them at 20p each and the small boys at his school snapped up this Oriental rarity. The dragon's eggs sold well, but this quick turnover was greatly assisted by the promise of deferred pleasure. The purchasers had been assured that the eggs would hatch in three weeks' time, when presumably the boys would become proud possessors of dragons.

A few weeks later a number of angry parents arrived at the home of my sculptor friends demanding the return of their sons' 20p. This was rightly refused because the boys had experienced the first thrill of collecting: the excitement of acquiring a mysterious object at a bargain price. The fact that it was no such thing also taught them their first lesson in collecting: don't do it if you can't bear the disappointment of discovering that the object is not so mysterious after all.

WHAT LADY DOCKER DIDN'T KNOW

JEWELS are a mystery. Take diamonds; I speak of large diamonds, of course. The sort that are given to women to pin on their chests. They are a controlled market and have little intrinsic value. Rarity lends them some merit; the pleasure they give makes them more prized. But neither attribute explains the mystery of diamonds, for the ingredients also include intangibles like danger, greed and lust – as these cautionary tales will tell.

One of the great collectors of her time was Nora Docker, the wife of Sir Bernard, who was chairman of BSA when it was still a great company. She collected people, parties and particularly publicity, and brought some light into the life of the newspaper-reading public in the dark days of the late 1940s and early 1950s, long before we were entertained by Page Three girls.

Towards the end of a long life as a professional celebrity, Lady Docker lived alone and largely unrecognized in the great Western Hotel in Paddington. One morning she was approached by a good-looking man in his mid-40s.

'Excuse me, but are you Lady Docker?' he asked.

'Yes,' she said.

'Please excuse me for saying this to you, Lady Docker, but since childhood I have always admired you. Since childhood I have always wished to meet you.'

'Oh,' said Lady Docker.

'Would it be impertinent to suggest that you lunch with me at the Ritz tomorrow?'

Now Lady Docker did not get too many luncheon invitations at this stage of her career. She accepted.

They had sat for a while at their table in the restuarant of the Ritz before the man took her bejewelled hand.

The luncheon seemed to be a great success. The man charmed Lady Docker and, more important, he seemed overwhelmed by *her* wit, *her* charm, *her* dress, *her* jewels.

'Could I see that ring, the diamond ring? You see, my trade is diamonds.'

Reluctantly she drew the ring from her finger. In a flash he had a jeweller's loop in his hand. He studied the jewel.

'Wonderful, wonderful,' he said. 'So fine, so fine, but I must see this jewel in natural light.'

In a moment he was gone. Poor Lady Docker was left, a little befuddled by champagne, without the ring but with a bill for lunch.

A tale of theft – a fear that haunts those who would collect fine jewels. Where jewels are concerned, there is always the suspicion of theft.

One Saturday morning long since, when the banks all opened as a matter of course, a young man entered a smart Bond Street jeweller and was shown a small chair and table to await a salesman. He glanced at his watch: 11.45 was the time.

'What can I show you, sir?'

'Diamonds.'

After a quarter of an hour, he chose a diamond for £5,000 – a very large sum in those days.

'Thank you, sir.'

'Here is my cheque.'

'You will collect the ring on Monday, sir?'

'No, I will take it now.'

'I am afraid, sir, that you are not known to us.'

'Ring my bank.'

The salesman went off to ring the bank and returned promptly. 'No reply,' he told the customer. 'The bank is closed.'

'Ring the Ritz Hotel.' (Why are these stories always set in the Ritz?) 'I've been staying there some months.'

The Ritz knew him well so he was able to take the ring with him on the short walk down Bond Street, and into the Ritz bar. 'A dry Martini, please, barman, and how would you like this ring for £500 that I have just bought for £5,000?'

Well, what would you do? The barman told the manager, who told the jewellers, who told the police, who arrested the man. When his cheque was cleared on Monday morning, all three got sued. He settled with the police, hotel and jeweller for a sum in excess of £5,000.

The subject of the last of these stories had no desire to make money. On the contrary; but it is a cautionary tale, nevertheless.

Just a few years ago a man entered the most famous of Bond Street's family firms. They knew this man and they would extend him no credit. He was not an evil man, just unreliable with cheques. When he visited their premises late on a Friday afternoon accompanied by a young woman of beauty – a quite stunning young lady – they were even more suspicious than usual.

Our man spent but a few seconds making his selection. In fact, he strode straight to the showcase with the large diamonds in it. He chose a fine diamond bracelet of top quality made by Cartier in the 1930s. In a moment he had it on the young lady's wrist. The family of jewellers stood like a rugby team, ready to impede her exit, but instead he turned and asked the price. £150,000, he was told.

'I will take it,' he declared.

'Hold on,' they said 'how will you pay?'

'With my cheque,' he said.

'You'll leave the bracelet here till it clears.'

'Of course, that presents no problem.'

And so turning, he kissed the stunning young lady, and removed the bracelet from her wrist.

'On Monday, my darling, we will collect it,' he said.

With a contemptuous smile he left the shop. The family of jewellers looked at each other and shrugged. On Monday, at three on the dot, he returned alone.

'I am afraid that I no longer require your bracelet.'

The family protested.

'Look boys, that sale made very little difference to you, but, for me, it made the most sensational weekend.' This also proves that, for collectors, diamonds are much more entertaining than mahogany commodes.

OF MEISSEN MEN

THE moment that tests a dealer's nerve comes after 4.30 p.m. on a Friday when an unknown customer offers a transaction that promises a profit so large that he would have to spend the whole weekend worrying about it. The experience goes like this: the customer asks for a sapphire, and is shown two, one of five carats and another of 25 carats. Naturally, he asks for one of 17.5 carats. He is shown a ring – perfect colour, 17.5 carats. He says it is wonderful and asks to borrow the dealer's hoop. He observes that the stone is of the very best quality. Not a mark on it. Exactly the right size. What a shame, he says, that it is a ring. Of course, he wanted a brooch.

'We will have it made into a brooch by Tuesday,' the dealer says. No good, he replies, he must have it today.

Because he is human, the rejection comes as a relief to a dealer in antiques, just as it would, in similar circumstances, to dealers in second-hand cars or brokers in money. Even so, this Friday customer is disturbing. After all, he might have spent a large sum and his cheque could have been cleared on the Monday.

This is why I have some sympathy for the dealer in, say, egg cups, who finds, on returning from a short holiday, that a customer has called at his shop and bought all his yellow egg cups. Since he has not sold a yellow egg cup in years, he might have missed a significant shift in the market.

Like any other, the antique market moves up and down, but it is uncommonly hard for a dealer to be sensitive to these movements all the time. The antique market is not like financial markets, there are no computers to record transactions. Newspapers do not publish daily the rise in Chippendale or the fall in Adam. There is no reporting of a bid for Chinese porcelain or a rights issue for Jacobite glass.

Many sales go unremarked, but the market is real enough. However, much as we may dislike the idea, antiques have become a form of currency – as legitimate as bronze bangles, cowrie shells or, for that matter, pieces of paper bearing the monarch's head and a facsimile signature of the Chief Cashier of the Bank of England.

Who would have thought that a rusting Mercedes-Benz could fetch £1.5 million? But why should a man not like a motor car by Benz 1/24th as much as a painting of some irises by Van Gogh that sold for £36 million. Perhaps more than any other, this market is susceptible to whim and dictated by fashion. Moreover, this fashion is distorted by nostalgia, chauvinism, and the prevailing view of what constitutes beauty.

A good example was the Phoenician exhibition at the Palazzo Grassi in Venice. (I have to say that the catalogue was more impressive than the sum of the exhibits. It probably weighed more than they did, too.) A small, but beautiful, glass bead in the form of a head was reproduced on the posters, enlarged from its real size of an inch to nearly a foot. This wonderful image caught the imagination of Venice and was reproduced in glass, china, papier mâché masks, posters and postcards. In the process, its price rose from a few hundred to several thousand pounds. The value, you might say, rose like a phoenix.

In the early 18th century, a Frenchman named Lemaire specialized in placing Chinese and Japanese porcelain on silver and gold mounts. He formed the view that it was not where the porcelain came from that mattered, but what it looked like. Consequently, he commissioned the Meissen factory to copy – at half the market prices – Japanese designs.

The customers admired the pieces greatly until they turned them over and observed the blue crossed-sword Meissen trademark. Since collectors wanted Japanese rather than German porcelain, the designs did not sell.

Lemaire approached the proprietors of Meissen, and explained that he had a small problem: it was difficult, he said, to sell these pieces with their trademark. Remove it, Lemaire said, and the stuff will go like hot cakes. The proprietors were appalled: Lemaire was saddened. But he refused to give up. Instead, he gave a few bob to the factory foreman, and said it was all right to put the crossed-sword mark on the porcelain – but only after it had been glazed. He then instructed a young man in his own establishment to rub the trademarks off. Lemaire's trade flourished. Without the Meissen mark, the pieces were marketable.

Only a few years later, factories all over Europe were pirating the Meissen trademark and selling a great deal of porcelain as a result. The market goes up and down, though when these tricks are discovered it is generally down.

But no market is predictable. Take so-called 'worthless bonds' –

issued by Tsarist Russia or a Peruvian railroad. Trade in them is brisk, and dealers scour the country for them. These bonds were money once, but having become worthless, their purpose changed. They were used, for example, to decorate lampshades. When these appear on the market now they are snapped up so that the bonds can be removed and restored. What began as money, and was transformed into an antique, becomes money again.

Breaks with the Past

In January 1988 the art market echoed to the sound of dealers expressing doubt. They kept up a front, of course, insisting that the stock market crash three months before had not affected their market. It proved their point, they said: works of art are a better investment than stocks and shares. They were right, there was no fall in saleroom prices. But there was no increase either. Dealers reassured each other, and then they reassured their clients, but the general view was that the coming year looked pretty tacky.

Only 12 months later the art world echoed to the sound of records smashing. One week in November a record was set for the number of records broken in one week. There was hardly an area where records remained intact. The market seemed to have moved up from a simple boom into a different sphere in which the value of objects and paintings was being assessed anew. Sales at Sotheby's and Christie's had the high profile, but the rise in prices was, perhaps, even more dramatic in provincial antique shops. It was no longer a surprise to find a local antique dealer asking £40,000 for a commode. This increase in values had spread through the whole country; the whole world as well.

What on earth had caused it? Inflation was the most common answer.

Inflation is sometimes the collector's friend, but I do not think inflation was the reason. I believe the rise was due to the increase in real wealth in Europe, the US and Australia that has resulted from the fashion for reducing taxation. This was combined with the spread of education, by which I do not mean that more people taught Latin and Greek, but that you could not switch on the radio or television, or pick up a newspaper or a magazine, without finding someone trundling on about what a good thing it would be if you bought some antiques.

Maybe it is just conceit, but I do believe that the accumulation of all this affected the price of paintings. I can recall a time when I had a Jackson Pollock hanging on my dining-room wall and none of my guests had any idea what it was. In fact, they would commiserate with my parents about my state of mind. Times have changed. I no longer have a Pollock on my wall, but if I had, the guests would spend half dinner discussing it. They know it is valuable. Therefore they assume it is good. Unfashionable Van Gogh has been transferred from John Betjeman's poetic bathroom to be hung, literally millions of pounds later, on the wall of a Japanese insurance company. [*The other is of course, referring to the first verse of Betjeman's* 'Winthrop Mackworth Redivivus'.]

More people understand art, or understand its implications. It is fashionable and since more people are rich, prices rise. In the US alone there are more than a million cash millionaires. Just suppose each of them wanted a single piece of English 18th-century furniture. Oh my! how the market would move.

There are always anomalies in rising markets, and glass is such an area. I know that people are nervous of glass, and it is certainly true that it has the habit of breaking when dropped. So does china, but that did not inhibit the rise in its price.

Before acquiring a magnificent collection of glass, you ought to heed this cautionary tale of a dealer in Paddington who moved up in the world. His new premises were magnificent and he took especial trouble with the window. He planned a display of columns in stone and plaster, each of different height, and on each he placed glass – decanters, jugs, bowls and drinking glasses. Completed, it looked wonderful.

Next, the dealer turned to a long oak table that he had placed by the wall next to the window. He planned to hang two pictures above the table, on which a pair of Irish fruit bowls would be displayed. He hung the first painting with ease. Disaster beckoned when he

began to hammer home the nail for the second picture. His blows caused the first picture to fall, and break an Irish fruit bowl. As its fall continued, the first picture knocked over the second picture, which was leaning against the table. That, in turn, fell against one of the columns. You can imagine the rest.

The new shop was a chaos of fallen columns and broken glass; a customer stepped over the rubble and shards to commiserate with the dealer, who said: 'It was a disaster that sort of crept up on me.' But it was not over. On inquiring of his insurers, the dealer was told that he had no brittles clause in his contract. The lesson of this story is that if you do not know what a brittles clause is, you should not collect glass.

Nunc Est Bibendum

SOTHEBY'S recently gave a dinner party for many of the leading wine writers. The meal was extraordinary, and so it should have been, for it was cooked by Michel Roux of Le Gavroche. The wine defied belief, let me record the list: champagne Krug 1982 followed by Haut Brion 1961 en magnum; Margaux 1953 en magnum; Latour 1952 en jeroboam (I asked the excellent gentleman from Château Latour why he chose this vintage, and he replied that Château Latour was most famous not just for great wines in great years, but for making good wines in bad years); Mouton Rothschild 1949 en magnum; Lafite Rothschild 1945 en jeroboam. All this finished off with Yquem 1970. Some of those present, may, but I doubt whether I will ever see the like again.

In the midst of all this – the dinner was held in Sotheby's main saleroom in Bond Street – stood the sculpture of the 'Dancing Faun' by Adriaen de Vries, unsold at that time but known to be of great value. Some weeks later it fetched £6.8 million, or about the price of a good-sized Jasper Johns. This comparison between the Renaissance and the 20th century seems to me to demonstrate what a bargain it was. In any event, the old couple from Surrey in whose garden it had stood for 30 years cannot have been displeased with the price – nor indeed the Chancellor of the Exchequer, who no doubt will have his cut. The King of Sweden, Carl Gustav, owner of 31 bronzes by de Vries, should be pretty pleased too. They decorate the garden of his palace at Drottningholm.

The old couple's windfall reminds me of a story which, I am told, emanates from the luncheon room at Malletts and was told by Frances Egerton, which means it must be true. In any event, a titled family sent three pictures to the auction rooms and they were sold one Thursday in the early 1970s – lots 161, 162, 163. The estimates were £10,000 for the three lots, split equally. The next day the wife rang the saleroom and was given the results. 'Lot 161' said the girl in Sotheby's. '£150,000.' There was a crash followed by silence. 'Hello; hello,' said the girl. Then a strange voice at the other end said 'Hello'. 'Who are you?' said the girl. 'I am Lord Whatever' said the voice. 'But I was speaking to your wife.' 'I know,' said Lord Whatever, 'but she has just passed out; you can give me the figures.' 'Lot 161,' said the girl, '£150,000' and then blurted out, 'Lot 162,

£300,000.' There was a louder crash at the other end of the line. 'Hello; hello,' said the girl. 'Hello; hello,' a strange voice replied. 'Who are you?' asked the girl. 'I am the gardener. Her Ladyship passed out and now I am afraid his Lordship has passed out as well.' 'Do you want the results of the sale?' said the girl. 'No, I think I had better call the doctor instead,' replied the gardener.

This just shows there is no such thing as an absolute value, a point wine illustrates as well as anything else. Christie's also recently asked me to drink some of their fine vintages, and since I was in a wine mood I waxed lyrical about the merits of wine. I remarked that I had seen a bottle of Cheval Blanc 1949, a superb wine, for £600. The lady on my left attacked my enthusiasm for this bargain: 'What extravagance.'

'But,' say I, 'we have just seen in the gallery of this auction house a beautiful Cézanne due to fetch £10 million. If you were to buy that painting it would cost you about £5000 a day in interest, you could buy a lot of wine for that.'

'Rubbish,' she replied, 'you drink your wine and it's gone, I still have my Cézanne.'

Rather weakly, I suggested that maybe she had worked out a way to take it with her when she had gone.

But the truth of the matter is that there are many types of collecting, and two are the collecting of the tangible and the intangible; each, I suppose, legitimate, each for quite a different sort of person. Of course, there are collectors who understand neither one nor the other.

Don't Look Twice

The summer in London is generally quiet; its inhabitants flee to distant lands in search of sun. No other season of the British year has such varied weather; you can drown, suffocate, freeze or broil on alternate days – sometimes even on the same day.

Nothing closes in London during August as it does on the Continent. On the other hand nothing is really open either. The shops lack proprietors: left in the hands of junior attendants who know they are not really expected to sell anything, they do their best to live up to expectations. The capital's great galleries show little in August that has not already been seen in June and July. The theatres are filled with Japanese audiences to whom the plays of the Western world are as intelligible as the Noh-play is to us. They laugh at sadness, applaud the mediocre and ignore the truly brilliant – making an evening at the theatre with them an eerie experience.

I made my way one summer to Sotheby's, who were exhibiting the work of the master carpenter John Makepeace and students from his school at Parnham. The work of the Master was not hard to distinguish from that of his followers. For a start he had far greater space to show his efforts. Then, while the students huddled amongst their offerings, the Master strode among his polished wood and metal chairs – which were smartly designed and beautifully executed. He also showed a cabinet that housed a model galleon, a breakfast table – its pedestal a bundle of saplings that appeared to grow from the ground – and a pair of chairs to go with it which seemed to owe more to topiary than carpentry. The plaster had a certainty of touch that separated him from his pupils; for example, a console table in blackened wood inlaid with coloured marquetry. This was an object that demanded great technical skill in its construction and was clearly a masterpiece of the cabinet maker's art – but not by any definition a work of art, not a masterpiece as we use the word today.

The word masterpiece was first used of the work an apprentice showed to his master in order to qualify in his master's trade – the best piece of work he had achieved. The word's meaning has changed, however, and a masterpiece is now considered to be a work equal to the best pieces achieved in any period.

Perhaps John Makepeace's students may feel I am unduly hard in my judgement of their efforts. 'I saw that man,' they might say, 'he only glanced at our work for a second or two.' How true these words would be; for a work of art to be a masterpiece, whether on canvas, in bronze, marble, silver or wood it must stop you in your tracks when your eyes light on it. For myself, I do not care what the thing is made of. I have been as impressed by a prehistoric circle of stones as I have with the great medieval cathedrals, as awed by a small painting of apples by Cézanne as by Veronese's *Feast at the House of Levi* – a painting more than a thousand times its size. They are both masterpieces. I am also as impressed with how Picasso used the handlebars of a bicycle as I am with the design of the bicycle itself, although neither of them are masterpieces – just examples of how a good design can be used in different contexts. (Personally I enjoy the stones laid in lines by Richard Long as much as I do the cave paintings of antiquity in Northern Australia – neither are masterpieces, but both in their ways are objects of beauty).

Something either *is* a masterpiece or it is not, there is no category in between. A work of art does not improve when looked at for great lengths of time, and it certainly does not become a masterpiece simply by being stared at. Nor do you discover how it became a masterpiece that way. I had a friend, now sadly dead, Sidney Nolan the Australian painter. At one time he spent several hours a day sitting and looking at the three paintings by Piero della Francesca in the National Gallery of London. Sometimes I sat with him. Many people, I suppose, would say that during that time he learnt about Piero and his paintings. For myself, I feel that while I sat and stared at these masterpieces I learned about myself. Sidney Nolan just enjoyed the work of Piero della Francesca – and had the National Gallery had ten of his paintings he would have divided his time between them.

No, masterpieces spring and strike the eye, grab you in the guts, leave you breathless with excitement. That is the time to start looking, thinking, comparing, searching for answers to questions such as: Does this piece have more than originality? Does it have moods that seem to change from day to day, qualities that transcend mere fashion? Furthermore the qualities that make masterpieces cannot be expressed in words. They are a form of communication in themselves, with their own language, and to be true masterpieces they must defy description by those who scribble.

Fakes Progress

THE fear that lurks behind the first major purchase of any collector must always be, is this minor masterpiece genuine? He or she draws reassurance from the dealer they buy it from, the position of his shop, the confidence with which he expounds on the history and the background of the piece, the books that he produces to show similar pieces. The more experienced collectors back their own judgement and sometimes become the greatest of experts. The most interesting collectors choose by eye. Is this piece the right shape? Is it aesthetically interesting? Is it beautiful? Is it ancient? This is the way to collect, but if you are impressed by professional expertise, go at once to the Victoria and Albert Museum, where there is a whole gallery of fakes bought by some of the world's greatest experts. If that gallery should not strike horror into your breast, then go to the bookshop of the British Museum, for they sell the catalogue of a fascinating exhibition of fakes that have been unmasked over the years, including a mermaid that I would give my eye teeth for. This mermaid must be a fake, for mermaids do not exist, or do they?

Of course, not all fakes are bad. In the British Museum's catalogue there is a carved panel, a 19th-century fake, but by chance, the fakers used a 15th-century altar panel, long lost, to make their fake. The painting on the back of the panel is of far more importance than the carving on the front would ever have been, even if it had been genuine.

Some fakes are made just for devilment. I remember a dealer in guns, Pip Roberts, now regrettably dead, who was shadowed in the salerooms by a man who, if you called him an amateur, would be an unjust slur on that fine status. However, if you called him a dealer, you would have to apologize to everyone who had ever sold an object in their lives. In any event, this man, when Pip Roberts raised his hand to bid, always went one bid more. He lived for some years off the expertise of my friend. In time, Roberts decided to teach him a lesson. Buying a Spanish gun of good quality for £50, for this was in the early 1960s, he inlaid it with silver and gilded the barrel, polished and carved it until it seemed like a masterpiece. Putting it in the saleroom, he waited for the auction and bid on it, bid and bid, casting glances of fury at his enemy. He was Italian, so you can imagine his antics as he bid, still higher. Suddenly he stopped. His enemy owned the gun at a very high price. In a matter of minutes everyone in the room knew the real story.

More recently, a man from the Middle East visited the showroom of a famous West End dealer to offer him a cuneiform tablet. As usual, the dealer asked him to leave it and he would show it to the museum. The man agreed. The museum was over the moon with excitement. The tablet was inscribed with a rare and complicated script, that would take a month to decipher, but it was well worth doing, for the tablet seemed of great interest and part of the first line said 'Nebuchadnezzar King'. The man from the Middle East returned and the dealer explained the delay.

'This is unacceptable,' came the reply, 'I have to return home tomorrow. I am afraid that I must take either my piece or the money.' The man asked a high price for the tablet.

'I'll pay,' said the dealer. The month passed and the museum rang.

'Rather funny really,' they said.

'What do you mean funny?'

'Well, there is a whole poem.'

I will not quote it all, but it will give you the gist of the thing if I say the poem is well known and it begins with 'Nebuchadnezzar King of the Jews' and ends with the 20th-century words 'the evening news'.

Some fakes are not fakes, or rather, they may not be fakes. At the moment, in the streets of Venice, there is a rash of men from North Africa selling luggage, supposedly fake, by the likes of Louis Vuitton and Gucci. Some Venetians believe these bags to be fakes while some believe they are genuine bags, stolen from the factories and being sold as fakes. In the end does it really matter much? If the object gives you pleasure, and if it is an object of beauty, this is what counts. If it happens to be a truly great object and genuine as well, so much the better.

What the Mind Doesn't Know

THIS story is set in an antique shop only a commode's throw away from Baker Street, which is appropriate because it is a detective story of a kind. This tale takes place in a different era, when antique shops kept large stocks of English and French furniture on the premises. Today's dealers are reduced to setting single pieces of furniture on Hessian covered plinths lit by five spot lights, but this tale happened in the early 1960s when stock was not short and prices were not high.

The item that interests us was not cheap. The dealer had a bureau bookcase in French black lacquer covered in ormolu. It looked like a masterpiece; and, better still, after consultation with the experts and research in great museums, it was found to have the provenance of a masterpiece. The pair to it was found in the Palace at Versailles; and it was not an obscure entry in the catalogue. The pair was in a position of honour.

Pieces of such merit are not easily found at any time, even in the early 1960s, and our man off Baker Street sent a telegram to the leading dealer in French furniture in New York: 'Masterpiece discovered stop pair in Versailles stop will hold till you arrive stop.' New York dealers are accustomed to telegrams like this and they don't just rush to London – however urgent the summons. This message arrived, however, at the end of June. July in New York is hot and sticky; July in London begins with the last week of Wimbledon. Consequently, the New York dealer bought four tickets for the *Queen Elizabeth* and told his wife and two daughters to pack. Evidently, the New York dealer was not breaking his neck to buy this unseen masterpiece. Indeed, he arrived at the Dorchester on a Friday and whiled away the weekend eating and drinking and watching tennis. He felt none of the energy and frustration that dealers feel when they are on the hunt. On Monday, he had a good lunch at Wiltons before setting off for Baker Street filled with good humour. When he entered the shop his eyes swept the stock and his humour changed.

'Where is my bureau bookcase?' he asked sharply.

The dealer's son took him back to the workshop, for in those days rents were low enough in central London for antique shops to take space for repairs and restoration. There he saw it. A bureau bookcase of the greatest quality.

'How much is it?' he asked.

'I'm afraid that it's reserved.'

'Reserved for me,' replied the New York dealer with a smile.

'No, for someone else. You did not come.'

'Get your father,' said the buyer, in that nasty manner that New York dealers have when things are not going their way. When the father arrived, he confirmed that he had news. The New York dealer exploded: 'I'll sue – for my time, the cost of my trip, the Dorchester, Wiltons, Wimbledon. I'll sue you for everything you've got.'

Before long, the dealer agreed to offer the anonymous purchaser of the bureau bookcase a profit and to resell the piece. While he was on the telephone, the New York dealer was offered coffee, and, as time went by, whisky. At last, the dealer returned with the problem resolved. The purchaser had agreed to take a profit. The price was higher and a protest was made. 'But I had it sold already,' said the dealer.

'I'll take it, subject to it being checked,' said the New Yorker.

So large was the sum offered for his advice that it took only two days for a great expert to arrive from Paris. He made a careful scrutiny and having carpenters take the piece apart, and once they had done so he declared it an astonishing discovery. There was no record of a pair having been ordered for the Palace of Versailles. Only one had been delivered, but this second example was quite genuine, the expert declared. The judgement was 'rare; very rare indeed'.

So, the deal was done, and the price was enormous, even for those days. His humour restored, the New York dealer returned home. He cabled the director of the Metropolitan Museum and made an appointment for him to view the bureau bookcase on its arrival in New York. The shippers were alerted, and arrived at the shop to take the bureau bookcase to the warehouse to be crated for its journey. They picked it up and lumbered towards the door, and got no further. No matter how they tried it would not fit through the door. Nor would it go through the side door or the back door. The awful truth about this bookcase was that if it could not be manhandled out, then it could not have been carried in. The bookcase was the masterpiece of the men who had worked most of their lives in the carpentry shed at the back of the shop.

I do not know what the New York dealer said; nor do I much care, for it was after all a masterpiece, and here is the great dilemma. For the antique-buying public it is quite clear that the old adage is true: what the mind doesn't know, the heart doesn't grieve for. Does it really matter whether an object is genuine?

To help you resolve this proposition, visit the gallery in the Victoria and Albert Museum that contains only fakes. I would be proud to have any one of them in my parlour. In this I may, perhaps, be accused of being somewhat permissive. For while I would say to the Baker Street dealer, were he still alive, that deluding other people can be tolerable, I would tell the New York dealer to beware of self-delusion because that is totally intolerable.

WHEEL OF FORTUNE

DURING the 1980s, summer in London was the centre of the art world; exhibitions and sales, cocktail parties and gallery openings. Comings and goings, and mostly it is the same people who come and go.

There are the dealers, and the good ones are like dealers in any other commodity. If, and only if, they have the ability, they make money whether there is a general boom or a general bust.

The admiring crowds gather round the old collectors who had the brilliance to acquire work by Barnett Newman or Jackson Pollock in the early 1960s (when the canvases were regarded as daubs of colour purchased by loonies).

The new collectors are less celebrated: they are the sort who buy 60 Schnabels and build museums to house them. The academics write about these new masters and beg a drawing in return. As for the artists, they are tucking into the canapés as if tomorrow's breakfast is an uncertain event. The wines are assorted and the drinkers mixed.

In June 1987 the second Van Gogh that year fetched a record, but another major sale had 30 per cent unsold. It was as if the art world had been turned into a casino, for everyone it was gambling.

In the midst of all this the Mark Rothko show opened at the Tate. His paintings are very pretty things – great shapes of colour. They are to decorate walls, and are not meant for carved and gilded frames. There is no story in these paintings; no chance among these great bands of colour of finding an ancestor.

Lurking behind these pictures of immense value is an intriguing scandal in the best tradition of this world of genius and big bucks, where passion can have motivations that do not spring from a love of beauty – passions like greed and corruption, for example.

In any event, Rothko died – by suicide in quietly dramatic circumstances. He lay in his bath and cut his wrists, the bathwater coloured by his blood. He left an estate of several hundred paintings to his family. At about this time I visited the New York gallery where he sold his work and when I mentioned my sadness at Rothko's death to one of the sales assistants, I was promptly offered some of his work, six paintings to be exact. The price seemed very reasonable. In fact, it was so reasonable that I could not resist the offer. In my ignorance I had always assumed that when some poor painter dies, the price of his pictures rises and someone else becomes rich. That was not so in this case. The prices seemed to have fallen.

This set of circumstances appeared strange. However, when I was joined by my purchases in London I felt really quite pleased with myself. So I showed them to an expert, boasting of the small price I had paid. 'There must be something wrong with them,' he said, and he turned the six pictures upside down.

Finally, he said: 'I can't see it.'

'What can't you see?' I asked.

'What's wrong with them.'

'Suppose nothing is wrong.'

'I know who you bought them from, and I know how much you paid. Something is wrong.'

I dismissed his suggestion as petty jealousy inspired by my bargain, but I'm afraid my friend, the expert, was right. A year or two passed, and then in my mail I received an invitation to travel to New York. It came from the district attorney, who wanted my presence in his office. I decided that I preferred to write.

After some months' correspondence I convinced him that I was merely a simple seeker after art of great beauty, especially at bargain prices, and that my part in the transaction was not at all evil. None the less, he declared that my evidence might be crucial in the complicated case he subsequently brought against Rothko's dealer, and one of the trustees of the estate. The reason it appears my Rothkos were such bargains was that these prices established a new market value at which the dealers would purchase Rothko's paintings from his heirs. These prices made them a bargain for him, too.

I explained to the district attorney that air travel was a problem for me, but that a liner sailed to New York every two weeks and that if he should purchase a first-class return ticket and obtain reservations for me at the Regency Hotel in Park Avenue, I would be delighted to attend on him in person. Unfortunately, as the cost of my trip escalated, the value of my evidence diminished. In the end the district attorney's man interviewed me at the Dorchester. He drank coffee, I drank tea.

The world of art is a wonderfully mixed place where philanthropy and crime rub shoulders and occasionally swap roles.

It is a world of excitement and disappointment, passion and commerce, and after having experienced the passion and the excitement, the disappointment overcame me when commerce dictated that I had to sell my Rothkos, in the mid-1970s at a time when the art market had taken a dip. Something had to go, and the objects that are easiest to sell are the best. Today my six Rothkos would be worth about $1 million each.

The lesson of this sad tale: speculate if you must, for it can be profitable and fun, but buy from the heart. If your paintings also happen to be bargains, don't pass them up. Although if they are like my Rothkos, try to hold on to them longer than I did.

For Better, for Worse

THE annual antiques fair at Grosvenor House is a truly great event, not so much because of the quality of the antiques but because this is the one place where you can be sure that they *are* antiques. Nowhere is the vetting committee more relentless in removing objects with even the hint of perfidy.

One year the antiques were on the whole diverse and beautiful, and the way they were presented was exceptional. Trusthouse Forte has a prize for the best decorated stall. A panel of a dozen or so decorators was chosen and set to cheer the place up; they succeeded mightily. The gentlemen from down the street at the Savoy who claim that Trusthouse Forte is good for nothing but portion control should have taken time to visit this *tour de force*.

There were more foreign dealers than before, all of them top quality. I found a surprising stand positioned between the two staircases, a stand that had the feel of a royal loan on display. It was no such thing. The showcase was filled with the best that Dutch dealers had to offer and any aspiring collector should, on this evidence, head for Amsterdam.

As to Olympia's antiques fair … I suppose it is unfair to mock the afflicted, but someone must tell them how truly awful it is, so awful that if I did not call it that I would have to apologize to every other undertaking to which I have applied the word. Perhaps I go too far; the catering was fine, with several discreet bars, each a different haven from all the awfulness.

I have been collecting all my life – everything from truncheons (18th- and 19th-century ones, the kind that policemen no longer have any use for) to rare breeds of chickens. I have toyed with collecting barbed wire, which is a popular activity in Texas; I have even thought of hoarding different styles of Coca-Cola bottle (the European chairman of the company has, as you might imagine, a large collection), which at their best fetch high prices and can be quite beautiful. In short, I am beyond redemption. But the Olympia fair came within an ace of causing me to give up, sell all and never collect again.

Of course, I did buy something. In fact I bought two items, both fakes. They were two of the famous, or infamous, 'Billies and Charlies', after the jolly London mudlarks who took the academics of the late 19th century to the cleaners. Now their work is much sought after.

The fair season over, there is now time for a cup of tea in the backroom at S.J. Phillips, Bond Street's most famous jeweller. Time to look at beautiful objects, to spot today's Billies and Charlies. There is no rush – I am a customer again rather than a victim.

Customers have to be handled in different ways. Some need pressure; the suggestion that if they fail to buy, another will, concentrates their minds. Others must be reassured and offered a profit, although they will seldom if ever take that profit. Some need to be pushed; and some need pulling.

Some years ago, an American in a Bond Street silversmith paid £10,000 for a Queen Anne coffee pot. This was a man of great means, well known in his industry.

'How lucky you are,' the shopkeeper said.

'Why?' the American asked.

'Queen Anne pots of this size and quality are hard to find.'

'Oh,' the American said.

'Nicely marked 1706.'

'1706?' the American said. 'Has this pot been in stock that long?'

'Lord no. It belonged to the dukes of Buckingham – look at this crest.'

'You mean it is second-hand?'

'Well, not the words I would use,' the shopkeeper replied. 'Antique, sir, and very lovely too.'

'Cancel the sale,' stormed the American. 'How could you expect my wife to use a second-hand pot.'

Customers are strange; but then so are dealers. Tessiers of Bond street was many years ago run by two brothers called Parson, one of whom was a bit of a wag. One day he was conducting a little business with the young Martin Norton from S.J. Philips, when an elderly lady and two dogs came in attended by a chauffeur. Parson nudged Norton:

'I'll show you how to deal with a customer, my boy,' he said. 'Good morning, madam. It's **** awful weather.' (He used a terrible swear word.) The young Norton, and the chauffeur, were shocked.

'Good morning, Mr Parson,' the lady replied. 'I think you have confused me with my deaf sister.'

In antique dealing it is the relationship between the dealer and the customer that is important. The art and antiques business is really about people, not objects. The interest and variety of people are infinitely greater than those of the objects. And each is more important than any object ever made.

ART À LA CARTE

THERE is hardly a restaurant or hotel in the world that does not have a picture or two in it, and the habit of placing paintings in commercial buildings has been growing for many years. The great skyscrapers of the world's capital cities have sculpture in profusion (often very good sculpture), and their foyers have paintings by contemporary artists; large because their foyers are large. Indeed, that is the way artists have preferred to paint in the last three decades – producing pictures far too big for most domestic premises. The bulk of these paintings and sculptures are of good quality. You even find the works of masters of the 20th century – Rothko, Henry Moore and Calder.

Hotels, however, are a disaster area for works of art – in London at least, from the merely bad, at the Hilton and the Royal Garden Hotels, to the totally disastrous at the Connaught. Who chooses these paintings is a matter of some fascination to me. I would love to meet that person if only to ask why such awful works are hung there. The Dorchester, The Ritz and Claridges make do with gold paint – there is no real attempt to introduce works of art. Have these proprietors no eye for art? I suppose the question answers itself when one visits their hotels, and the answer is a resounding NO.

Mark Birley, on the other hand, the proprietor of three of London's best restaurants, has an extremely good eye for paintings. But then he should, being the son of a considerable portrait painter. Annabel's has an interesting selection of pictures ranging from Matthew Smith to Munnings, Mark's Club has a collection of Victorian paintings, and Harry's Bar a selection of posters and an enormous collection of original cartoons by Peter Arno. The taste in all these places is extremely personal – and extremely good. If you wish to eat *and* look at pictures, however, the only place to go is to the Garrick Club, which has the world's largest collection of theatrical paintings. Several of these are by Zoffany; some are good and all of them interesting. As for the food – well, the members of the Garric Club go there for the conviviality of their fellow members and their guests; looking at the pictures takes your mind off the food.

The National and the Tate Gallery are both places were you can eat and look at paintings. Both galleries are stuffed full of masterpieces, but their restaurants are another thing. The Tate Gallery has a mural by Rex Whistler. The National Gallery in its fine new extension has a large mural by Paula Rego; not the sort of work of art that sticks in your mind – far better to miss lunch and spend the time walking round their galleries looking at the paintings and sculptures. In the Tate Gallery there is one room of paintings that were once destined to be hung in a restaurant; the paintings are by Rothko, and they were painted for New York's Four Seasons restaurant. Why they were not hung there is obvious when you stand with them in the Tate – their quiet beauty is overpowering. Painted towards the end of Rothko's life, they have a deep sadness about them – objects of the greatest quality, they are not at all the sort of works that would go well with the clatter of cutlery and the clink of bottles, let alone the idle chatter of fashionable New York as it consumes its food. These are silent and reflective pictures suited to the place where they are hung. Why anyone has to eat in a museum at all is a mystery to me – far better to get rid of all these restaurants in our public galleries; to give up catering and show more pictures, which, after all, is what they are there for.

There has always lurked in the minds of those who would open restaurants an idea that hanging pictures will attract clients who believe that they will be able to watch the artists whose work hangs there eat. This occasionally works. The Neal Street Restaurant has the work of Hockney and Richard Smith – but then they had the good fortune to have Kasmin, the remarkable West End art dealer, as a shareholder. They also had a large painting of a mushroom by Sidney Nolan, which was there, I think, because Antonio Carluccio likes Nolan's work, and both he and Nolan like mushrooms. The Ivy Restaurant has work by Howard Hodgkin and Allen Jones – and the artists themselves can be seen there.

These restaurants and their paintings are all very well in their way, but they cannot compete with the Colombe d'Or in Saint Paul de Vence – a restaurant that collected art 40 years ago. The collection that this restaurant has is magnificent – major works by Chagall, Picasso, Miró, Léger and by a great many other artists as well. Whether or not the likes of Picasso paid for their food with paintings I do not know, but I can remember in the early 1950s sitting on the terrace of that restaurant looking down over the then beautiful valley – at terraces of olive trees and the occasional row of vines. White doves sat in the lemon trees, and I watched as Chagall and Picasso sat with the friends and ate their lunch – in those days lamb or chicken cooked on a spit and served with salad. At that time their pictures were the butt of jokes among ignorant people: Munnings said over dinner at the Royal Academy, 'If Picasso comes to London I will kick him in the pants.' Picasso replied 'Who is this Munnings?' The paintings still hang in the Colombe d'Or – Picasso and Chagall are gone. The valley is crammed with holiday homes; the pictures? – worth very much more; the food? – no longer good.

DECORATING TROPHIES

PROPRIETORS of hotels and restaurants all have different ideas as to what kinds of decor will bring in customers – the proprietors of pubs for that matter have strong views too. As a theatrical friend of mine once said: 'You have to give the customers something to make them cross the road.' What most owners of eating and drinking establishments provide does just that for me – but in the opposite direction. Every once in a while you come across a proprietor who has succeeded in getting the decor of their premises exactly right. The Old Mill, a pub at Dipley in Hampshire, was run by one of these. Not a grand public house with oak furniture and horse brasses, this was a one-room pub. The door from the road entered into that one room. It was a small room and the bar ran the length of one side of it. Behind the bar stood Mrs Crate; small like the room, she could scarcely be seen over the top of the bar. On the shelves behind stood her collection, a row of spongeware mugs. Some of these mugs had been used in her pub a hundred years ago for drinking beer, others had been collected as they were discarded by the other proprietors who changed to glass tankards. In the middle of this display was an old photograph of the yard behind the mill, where on Sundays, a game was played that involved throwing small cast-iron discs. There were several of these discs on the shelf, but the pride of Mrs Crate's collection were half a dozen extremely ancient bottles of Newcastle Brown Ale, each bottle garlanded with plastic flowers. The whole display was never dusted. Sadly, Mrs Crate is now dead, her pub sold and her collection dispersed.

In London there was another such place, different, but a place that with its contents had the imprint of its owner's personality – the Cavendish Hotel. This was the old Cavendish Hotel that stood in Jermyn Street on the site where now a new hotel stands. I never met Rosa Lewis, who was the owner of that first Cavendish Hotel, but I did visit her premises after she died and before it was pulled down. Rosa Lewis made a speciality of providing what she loved to call 'nice clean young girls' for the English gentry or visiting Americans. She also made a penny or two by selling antiques to the rich Americans while they were either intoxicated by liquor or the charms of the 'nice clean young girls'. Maybe she acquired these antiques from the English in lieu of cash for the services of the nice young girls. In any event, her hotel was filled from basement to attic with antiques. I remember, as the hotel stood almost empty ready for the demolition men's hammers, there remained just one object, an object so large that no one knew how it had got there in the first place, and certainly none of the Americans who had bought and paid for this object had ever been able to arrange to have it removed. The object was an archway, a large stone archway. The building was pulled down around it and was free. The archway came originally from Dorchester House, the mansion that once stood where the Dorcester Hotel now stands. Why Rosa Lewis bought it remains a mystery. There must surely have been more manageable objects available to deal in. That she never paid for it remains a fact, but that was the nature of the woman.

By chance I was travelling in Sweden and I visited Stockholm. I found myself booked into a hotel with the unpromising name of Victory. I expected a clean and soulless hotel, the sort designed to cure tourists of the tiresome habit of wanting to travel – how wrong I was. The Victory is indeed part of a chain – a chain of hotels owned by Gunnar Bengtsson, a true collector in the mould of Mrs Crate and Mrs Lewis. His other two hotels are called The Lord Nelson and The Lady Hamilton. This man is obsessed with Nelson. He collects everything that has even the loosest association with that Admiral, or is Mr Bengtsson just a collector and Nelson a vehicle he issues to satisfy that need? For Mr Bengtsson sought out a very large collection of late 19th- and early 20th-century ship paintings and, not content with this, he found photographs of the captains who commanded them. His three hotels are filled – literally – with collections: boxes, pipes, toys, Swedish furniture and anything nautical, from ships in bottles to bottles of wine that come from ships. Gunnar Bengtsson is still alive and still collecting. He recently bought Nelson's home, Trafalgar House, in Wiltshire. Many other proprietors try to furnish their hotels with antiques but few know how to succeed because the hotels only pretend to have antiques – as so many antiques only pretend to be antiques.

A Chequers Past

OLD politicians call it Chequers weather: the sun that shines unseasonably on the gardens of the Tudor mansion that presides at the end of a long valley in the Chiltern Hills. Hills rolling towards a great escarpment that looks out over Buckinghamshire towards Oxford and Aylesbury. Hills capped with tall beechwood, a valley with a winding road and flocks of sheep grazing in the field. A dream of rural England, a house given to the nation by Lord Lee of Fareham in 1917 for use by our prime ministers to entertain visiting foreign dignitaries, a country residence.

The world has its great houses and England has far finer, far grander houses than Chequers, but there is no house that so exactly expresses England and the English: the English art of understatement. Never, I suppose, do strangers to our land quite understand it. Never do they understand why it is that they are impressed when shown so little with which to be impressed. This house, this valley, marshalls thousands of years of history and is not ashamed to boast of it. That history is in the bricks, it is in the land, it is in the great beech trees and you feel it. History at your elbow as you drive through the Churchill Gate (opened only for visiting foreign heads of state, lesser men enter by the bothy at the side). History is there as you stand at the door.

This day was different from any other day. The date was Sunday 6 May 1979. The Prime Minister who had just come to office the previous Friday was different from her predecessors, for she was a woman. Many years later, after she had left office, her record makes her different without doubt from the vast majority of her successors. And her personality – her critics seem in one accord that it is her personality alone that has changed much.

Chequers had not been left untouched in these changes. On that Sunday she entertained a group of her ministers to lunch. Amongst them were Lord Thorneycroft, the Party Chairman, and myself, appointed his deputy the day before. The sun shone on the line of black ministerial cars that drove to the front door. There was an air of excitement, perhaps even of triumph, amongst these men. They were returned to office. Some of them had known Chequers in the days of Churchill, some in the days of Heath. Others, like myself, had never been there before. Drinks before lunch in the Hawtrey Room, filled that day with nervous laughter and loud voices.

Lunch, truly terrible food, with its now famous tale of Sir Geoffrey Howe and the lamb chops variously reported as a whole tray in his lap to a little gravy on his lapel. At any event, it is true that the Prime Minister did jump up and comfort the WRAF lady who had spilt whatever it was, leaving the wretched Sir Geoffrey to his own devices. I suppose this event set the scene for Mrs Thatcher's relationship with her staff at Chequers and, for that matter, with the man who played a key part in bringing her down.

Coffee on the terrace; small groups of ministers stood and talked, the more elderly sat on the wooden benches. The first roses were beginning to appear and the clumps of herbaceous plants, overgrown as is often the way in mature English gardens, were just showing colour. The new Prime Minister moved from group to group, taking a minister to talk with her walking amongst the roses, sometimes calling on another colleague to join them, watched always by the assembly on the terraces, curious for any reaction, any hint of what was being discussed. The sun shone on that garden, even on the new indoor swimming pool built by Edward Heath, obviously an enthusiast for swimming if not for architecture, a monstrous building owing, I suppose, its origins to the Georgians, while the house is inspired by earlier centuries. That day even this intrusion on a strange but impressive garden seemed tamed, a kind of joke about the past.

Heath's hand had left its mark on Chequers – John Fowler had been hired to decorate many of the rooms; but Harold Wilson and James Callaghan had not used the house that much. The place had an institutional feel, the atmosphere of a government building. John Fowler's work had been changed, pictures rehung, furniture moved from room to room, nothing seemed to be where it should be. The haircord carpets of the Long Gallery with its Fowler wallpaper (the same pattern that was first used in Annabel's, the Berkeley Square club), the painted panelling, it all seemed very odd. The poor arrangements of flowers, the electric fires.

I think that it must have been that weekend that Mrs Thatcher fell in love with this ugly, old house and, with this love, things began to change not fast, but remorselessly. No great armies of painters and decorators, no vast spending of money, but carefully phased. The changes came, log fires and flowers, the finding of paintings tucked away, brought out and rehung, better paintings given prominence, monsters carefully hidden. The house began to live, visitors were shown the house and its treasures often not by a guide but by the Prime Minister herself. The skylight in the dome of the great hall, boarded up years before, was unboarded and the sun encouraged to enter. The food became better, the chef began to appear in the dining-room to receive applause for his efforts. The treasures: the ring that Alec Douglas-Home's ancestor took to Scotland to give authority to the request to James VI of Scotland that he become James I of England; the table on which Napoleon signed his surrender. Cromwell's portrait; the painting of a great lion held in a net where Churchill had painted in a small mouse to chew its ropes. Souvenirs from past prime ministers and tales of their doings at Chequers. She understood the history of this house, and the house responded. For me, I remember the great Christmas tree decorated by the staff – she understood the house's traditions and encouraged them. Boxing Day. I recall sitting in the Long Gallery with its fine library, peacefully reading.

Times have changed. The uniformed police officers of that sunny day in May have been replaced by officers in flak jackets and heavy calibre rifles. The more events have conspired to restrict and change life at Chequers, the more Mrs Thatcher worked so that this house should be a family house. In her time there was much laughter there, much happiness. Fear and tension, too, when cabinet meetings were held at the time of the Falklands War. This house had changed, it was no longer like some club moved from London, thick with smoke of cigars, port and long, male sojourns in the dining-room, with bored women sitting in the Hawtrey Room and tired staff in the pantries. This was never her style. Chequers had become a family home where life was conducted with consideration and dignity, sympathy and always joy. In the last weeks of November 1990, if Mrs Thatcher shed a tear, it was not for the loss of position – rather perhaps for the leaving of a house that she had grown fond of, almost certainly for the parting from the staff of her official residence who, over nearly twelve years, she had come to love.

ERMINE AND EARLS

THERE is something strange about the House of Lords. Not its entrance – a modest entrance given the size and purpose of the place; not the policeman who guards the door – he is much like other members of the constabulary; not the doorman in his red coat and top hat, nor even the gentleman who stops you once you get inside, politely enquiring for whom you have called. The strangeness is in the cloakroom, that long, wide passage with its rows of coat hooks, where their lordships hang their coats: simple brass hooks, except, of course, the one where the Prince of Wales hangs his coat – though he seldom comes to the House of Lords, and when he does I am sure he has someone to look after his coat; even so he has his peg – *all* of the 1171 lords temporal have a peg and on many of them a coat hanger. The range of coat hangers is most remarkable – from the padded Harrods hanger of a recently enobled industrialist through the offerings of Savile Row and off-Savile Row tailors to the bent wire hangers so popular as motorcar wireless aerials. In summer these all hang like so many bones on a skeleton, in winter, they are fleshed out with an amazing range of coats.

The mock gothic House of Lords building is grand – to do it justice, it is very grand. Not so the contents; the peers by and large are a friendly lot, and conduct their business in the chamber in the most courteous of manners. Insults are rare, and the mildest of them is speedily followed by an apology. I recall a baroness, a junior minister, telling the opposition spokeswoman on some subject or other that she should 'grow up' – hardly the most devastating of verbal assaults, but the whips moved about the chamber and there was much whispering. Sure enough, the minister rose to apologize. Each point of disagreement is framed by an apology for differing with the idiotic statement just made: you can tell the House of Lords from the Other Place – which is how their lordships refer to the House of Commons – because apart from everyone being *so* nice to each other, all the benches in the chamber are red. When you cross the divide between the two houses everything changes: in the Commons, all is green.

Their lordships dress as befits their status – mostly in dark greys. I was once taken to task by an elderly peer for wearing suede shoes – 'Suede,' he said, 'is not worn here'; he added: 'I am surprised that the whips have not spoken to you before about this.' Often, because

I have the habit of wearing couduroy suits, I have been asked, 'Are you off to the country?'

The peers do quite a lot of 'hanging around'; unlike the Commons, votes in the Lords happen at any time of the day or night. The place where it is most congenial to hang around is the bar that used to be the Bishop's Robing Room – the room that once held clerical robes now holds their lordships engaging in a drink while waiting to troop through the lobbies. Off it is a small room serving the best food in the house – all fried: eggs, bacon and sausages, proper food for a hungry peer. For guests, the peers' dining-room serves lunch and dinner, but tea-time is the high spot of that room's repertoire. Forget lunch or dinner and save up for tea; two kinds of tea, Indian and China, anchovy toast, crumpets, muffins, sandwiches (egg, watercress and cucumber), and then the cakes, best of all a toasted teacake covered in melting butter; now this really is a place to spend one's time. After tea the library, a room filled with working peers and a few asleep in the deep red-leather armchairs, their feet resting on red-leather footstools, the day's newspapers fluttering on their chests as they gently suck in and expel the warm air. Startled into wakefulness by the clamour of the division bell, they adjust their dress and trundle off to pass through the lobbies.

This house first sat in 1295; it was called the model parliament and consisted of 140 lords, 2 archbishops, 70 abbots and priors, 8 earls and 41 barons, called together by Edward I. Since then it has changed a lot – there are now fewer churchmen and more hereditary peers, and of course since 1958 life peers. A dozen or so life peers are made each year. (Occasionally a few hereditary peerages are also granted.) These new peers are summoned to the house on a particular day, and have lunch in the dining-room with their family, a few friends and their two sponsors, who stand either side of them as they are introduced to the House, where they will take the oath of loyalty to the monarch. After lunch the new peer and his sponsors stand for photographs in their robes, the Garter King of Arms gives them a lecture on the ceremony that will follow and, feeling slightly ridiculous in their exotic outfits, they rehearse in the empty chamber – so many paces this way and so many paces that way, so many bows here and so many salutes there. The House sits and the new peer enters the chamber. It is at this moment that he feels the full majesty of that institution – the ranks of peers, the Chancellor in his wig and robes, the gilded chamber, this is a moment that cannot be forgotten. In that moment it becomes clear that an institution which could easily be seen as ridiculous is deeply important.

A Stock Solution

THERE is much talk about allowing museums to sell off duplicate or surplus works of art. Richard Luce, when he was our Minister for the Arts in 1988, announced his intention to make these sales easier. In museums, this process is called de-aquisitioning. I call it uncollecting, because no work of art has a duplicate. Even coins and stamps vary from one specimen to another.

Moreover, what is surplus to one museum curator may be a treasure to his successor. That makes the valuation of objects proposed for de-acquisition a subjective judgement: who decides how much the allegedly surplus or duplicate item ought to be worth? That is a difficult business, and there is a story that illustrates this problem, concerning the famous London dealer, Wertheim, a man much to be reckoned with in Bond Street circles in the early years of this century.

As Wertheim grew old his bones began to feel the cold and his sons wanted to buy him a warm coat. Wertheim, who seldom spent a half-penny if he could avoid it, resisted. Nevertheless, his sons clubbed together and bought a coat of the finest fur and, since it had cost no less than £500, they began to contrive a way of giving it to their begetter without provoking his anger. So, on returning from a country sale one day, they simply produced the coat and declared they had procured a great bargain for their father.

'How much?' the elder Wertheim demanded of them.

'Only £25,' the sons replied.

'Rubbish,' cried their father.

'It's not worth £12 10s (£12.50). Not even that.' But the sons were happy, for their father had a coat, and, privately, so was their father, for he had a bargain. He paraded in it up and down Bond Street.

One day he met Martin Norton, proprietor of S. J. Phillips, a shop still filled with good jewellery and antique silver, that was then the repository of much hospitality and many a good story. Norton admired his friend Wertheim's coat. 'How much did you pay for it?' he asked.

'Only £25.'

'I'll give you £50.'

'Done,' exclaimed Wertheim, and thus was a £500 fur coat sold for £50.

This story illustrates the illusion of profit, and leaves me with some doubts about the wisdom of allowing one set of museum curators to sell what has been purchased by its predecessors.

Our great museums are faced with many problems, not least a shortage of space. Indeed, they are short of the space to store their collections, never mind to display them. Something must be done, but before accepting random de-aquisitioning, I would like to propose an alternative.

To begin with I would introduce a radical measure to cancel the existing system of purchase grants to the museums. My system would be based on the simple method adopted by collectors through the ages doing swaps. I should require curators to list the objects they are willing to let go and circulate the list to all the other museums. Should a museum director in, say, Newcastle, wish to acquire an object on the British Museum's list, that object would be transferred from London to the North-East. A value would be attributed to the piece and the British Museum would receive a Treasury grant of corresponding value that could then be used to finance a fresh acquisition.

I assume that most of the traffic would be from the great national collections to museums in the provinces, thus encouraging them to acquire more works important to their collections while thinning the stock in the great storehouses of London. This practice would also guarantee that these works of art remained within our museum system, which, in turn, helps to persuade donors to give their collections to museums without the fear that unsympathetic museum directors in the future will simply flog them. Imagine how much more difficult it is to secure gifts if patrons know these can later be de-acqusitioned at the will of some anonymous trustees.

Perhaps because I am writing this in Venice, I am more sensitive to the problem, since the Venetians managed to de-aquisition so much of their own rich collections – greatly to the advantage of the National Gallery and the royal collections.

We do not need to look outside our own island for a cautionary tale. If you examine the manuscript copy of the catalogue of the collection of Charles I you will see, among all the treasures, lists of Titians, Raphaels, and Giorgiones. At the time it was the world's greatest collection of Renaissance paintings.

The royal collection also included King Alfred's crown, but the paintings were sold on the continent and the crown melted down at the Mint. This wonderful collection was turned into cash to meet the payroll of the Commonwealth armies. When it comes to de-aquisition, Oliver Cromwell is our champion. And look what happened to him.

Re-formist Tendencies

The motives of collectors are many and various, but I observe that greed is the dominant emotion. So I have looked, instead, for a few examples of generosity, such as a case in Julfar, in the Arabian Gulf, where a blue and white Chinese dish was found. Or, more accurately, the greater part of the dish. Having been restored, this fine dish was put on display in the Ras Al Khaimah museum, where a visiting collector noticed that the missing piece was a fragment that he had acquired himself some years previously. He donated his fragment to the museum, which now displays a fine and complete Chinese dish.

Museums are beginning to behave in the same way, and there is plenty of scope for reuniting works of art that have been broken up and sold around the world. A dramatic example of this is a 15th-century altar-piece of the Virgin and Child enthroned among angels by Benazzo Gozzali. Five predella panels from this altar are known to exist. The death of St Magnus is in the Royal Collection; the miracle of St Dominic is in the Brera in Milan; the miracle of St Zenobius in Berlin; the dance of Salomé and the beheading of John the Baptist is in the Kress Collection in Washington; and the Purification of the Virgin is in the Johnson collection in Philadelphia. How grand it would be if they were all put together, as the artist intended.

This proposition is, however, fraught with problems. Forget the owners; the scholars would forever be arguing whether the fifth panel really was part of the set. Armour is easier, for there is less room for debate. One suit of armour was made for the Duke of Urbino by Bartolommeo Campi of Pesaro about 1550; this is now scattered, with the visor in the Wallace Collection, London, other parts in the Bargello, in Florence, and still others elsewhere. The Bayard armour is in the Royal Armouries, London, and in the Musée d'Armeée, in Paris. The Sachsen–Altenburg armour is spread among the Royal Armouries, the Victoria and Albert Museum, Nuremberg, Dresden and elsewhere in Germany. There is room for some swapping by collectors of armour.

UK museums do not always follow this principle. Often they are reluctant to swop – or they might say exchange – works of art. Certainly, for many years the Egyptians have been trying to persuade the British Museum to return the beard of the Sphinx.

The Sphinx was built in about 2600 BC; almost 1,200 years later, in the 18th dynasty, the future Tuthmosis IV dreamed that if he uncovered the Sphinx and gave it a beard he would become pharoah. He did so, and his dream came true.

The beard was made of sandstone, and in time it fell off. It was bought quite legally by the British Museum in the 19th century, though I wonder why, for apart from being a great curiosity, it is of no real value. In fact, it is an ugly bit of stone about 4 feet long (it is not even the whole beard; other parts of it are still in Egypt). I do not see much point in putting it back on the Sphinx since it is a later mutation of the original work of art. However, the Egyptians do, and despite the fact that it has never shown it, the British Museum refuses to give it back.

The field is crammed with argument and counter-argument. Would the sculpted relief from above the door of the Scuola Vecchia by the Misericordia be better off back in Venice than being kept at the Victoria & Albert Museum, which acquired it in 1892, for example? The debate is endless, but at least it is under way. Art is being viewed as the property of the world, and selfishness is being exposed as a variety of greed. Is it plain greed that makes so many collectors buy only when the price of a work of art has been established? Is it greed that makes them scramble for the work of recognized masters, forcing the price even higher? Why do they neglect new young artists? Three-quarters of the world's wealthiest people collect art seriously, but I wonder how many buy a painting because it catches their fancy, or how many would dare to fill a drawing room with paintings that none of their friends could recognize.

Not all auctions are like Christie's, or conducted by the Hon. Charles Allsopp of the seductive hammer. The auctions held in the Royal Horticultural Hall in Vincent Square by the British Iris Society are a far cry from this. They are held several times a year and collectors bring their plants wrapped in plastic bags. Many of them arrive on motor cycles, and when the plants and the collectors are unwrapped, the plants are laid on a long table. The bidders sit round it and the auctioneer calls out: 'What am I bid? Fifty pence?' Five hands go up. 'Sold,' cries the auctioneer, and divides the lot into five parts. No one pays very much and no one goes away having bought nothing. Everyone seems pleased, perhaps because the one motive that is entirely absent from the occasion is greed.

Blooming Good Riddance

Right through the 1970s and 1980s flower arranging grew in extravagance, finally reaching a peak with the creation of trees out of sea shells; great arrangements of fruits; coloured mosses made into swags and bows and montages that covered the walls made of disused garden implements – implements heaped in a shed, implements of no account until taken out and carefully arranged in London apartments – a sort of dubious salute to a rustic world long gone and now inhabited by electric hedge trimmers and the like. With the beginning of the 1990s the time had come for a change of style.

Flower arranging had, people believed in those booming years of the 1980s, an honest, simple beauty. They talked of the integrity of the materials: nothing man-made; or, if he had made it, he did so out of clay or wood. The fashion was for bunches of flowers, but only one sort of flower, and preferably a simple country one tied with raffia, pushed into a crude pot or industrial glass vessel as though no thought had gone into this casual arrangement, when the truth was that an immense amount of thought *had* gone into it. The use of five times too many flowers in a vase bought at five times the right price. These were rich years and flowers were one of their more attractive aspects. Old wooden seed trays, the rougher the better, were planted with rows of the most elegant of tulips ready to flower simultaneously. Those years of plenty created, in flower arranging, a sort of fake poverty.

A change has come. The bills of florists who thrived during that prosperous period are now being carefully checked. There is a new style in floral decoration: no more clever arrangements of mosses. No more clay pots wrapped in raw linen. No more acid jars filled with great bouquets. Economy is the word these days, and flowers will be chosen with care. No florist will be allowed to pass on blooms at the end of their careers. Today's customer for flowers wants them firmly in bud. Now it is one branch of lilies that is put in a vase, along with the leaves of *Magnolia grandiflora* or some other long-lasting evergreen, and very likely the stalk of lilies will only be changed when the last flower has dropped.

Today the vases need to be different. Flowerpots are back in the garden, seed boxes have become tinder, and don't bother with raffia. Attics have been raided and the vases that some great-aunt brought back from Murano, the ones that once seemed so awful, have been brought out. If these vases from Murano are not good enough for Sotheby's or Christie's, then they are just right for flower arrangements: for the small vases, posies made up of all sorts of odds and ends, and as one odd or end dies it is replaced with another, for large vases use foliage – long-lasting foliage.

Thought is being given to the flowers themselves now the extravagance of the past is, for the moment, gone. Because flowers are being used singly or in small bunches, there is a need for stronger, brighter, harder colours. Gerberas, for many years a sort of joke flower, their petals used on hats – flowers that really look like flowers – these are the flowers for today. Roses, not the delicate pastel shades of the old-fashioned rose, but the hard, vibrant colours, Mr McGready's roses of the 1950s.

More care has to be taken with the choice of flowers. The sloppiness of the old-fashioned rose, where you could pick a basketful and no single colour clashed with any other, those days are gone. The roses of the 1950s need careful thought: a few to a vase and plenty of foliage. In recession people turn to plants that really last, not gardenias and orchids that need expensive hot houses, but cacti. These exotic plants come in thousands of varieties. The large ones form horticultural sculpture in a room; they withstand the central heating and benefit from a forgetful attendant. Should you tire of them, shuffle them around the house. Bonsai: they look wonderful as well, but are plants for the enthusiast. When you become hooked on tinkering with your collection of bonsai, holidays are lost. Leave these valuable little trees in the hands of someone else? Never! Arrangements of flowers? Not in the house of a bonsai lover, there is never any room.

Houses are changing to suit their owner's way of life. The last years have been years of change and disturbance, from Berlin to Abu Dhabi. These are years of reassessment: the year to clear rubbish, jettison the unwanted, decide what you really need. That piece of junk bought for so much in Chelsea at the end of 1989 looks just like a piece of junk. Take it to the saleroom and find that it is worth about as much as it looks. Houses will be clearer, decor harder and sparser, and the arranging of flowers will follow that pattern.

WHEN SHABBY MEANS CHIC

To many of us the romance of the slightly derelict landscape, or the once grand but now decaying house, has a strong attraction. Seeing this, decorators and dealers have promoted the crashed look, with carpets short on colour and long on holes, newly 'distressed' furniture and walls painted to imitate the effect of decades of tobacco smoke or crumbling plaster. The broken statue becomes an object of beauty, although if it is to be an art object, the break must be in the right place. This is a look with a little dust, but no dirt.

Objects look better when they acquire a patina, and the same is true of houses (even of people). Perhaps this is most true of gardens. The best are unkempt but never neglected. Bosky gardens celebrate the art of extraction. The principle is, if it looks wrong, pull it out. No clever placement of plants, just the luck of nature aided by the gardener. Time is caught still, the stone roller, the broken wheelbarrow are seen as if through a cobweb. The plants and trees seem rebellious and unconfined, with a life of their own.

Neither is such a garden the domain of the lazy. It is a stage set arranged with care to look careless. The right type of weed has to

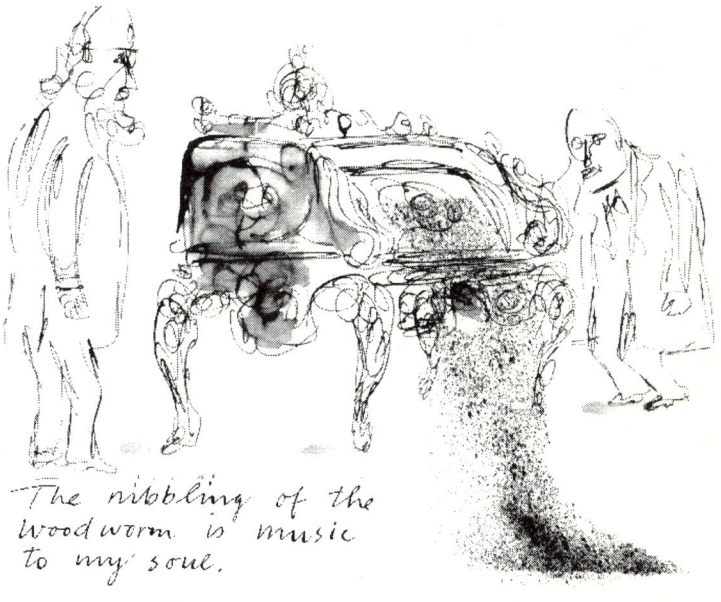

The nibbling of the woodworm is music to my soul.

be exactly chosen – and not too many of them – and the small wild dog roses are planted so that they seem to dance with old roses the size and shape of ball gowns. This is not so much the perfect garden as the secret garden, best in early morning or at dusk. Bright sunlight is not unknown, but it must be seen to come there only in patches – staining the stonework. Just as in a house the paint must peel but the timber never rot, there can be moss in the gravel but never weeds in the lawn. Incidentally, this reminds me of a British Ambassador to Japan some time past, who knew about lawns with no weeds, and instructed his Japanese gardener to pull them all out. In fact, he instructed him several times with little result. Finally, he said: 'I shall be away on leave for six weeks and if the lawn is not weeded by my return I shall be most displeased.' It was. True to Japanese tradition, the gardener had pulled out all the grass and left only daisies and other weeds.

Buildings are the same. The tired look is the fashion. I am, however, prepared to bet that the vast majority who greatly admire our medieval cathedrals would cry out with anguish at the suggestion that we should restore them to their original colours – garish colours, painted not only inside but all over the outside walls as well. Public taste, while claiming to admire past centuries and despise the look of our own age, does not, in fact, much like things to be presented as they really are. A fine example of this was once seen in a Frans Hals exhibition at the Royal Academy. The show was worth seeing for the pictures, but I was most interested in the frames: old gold, new gold, frames encrusted with smoke, frames stroked by time till they became a gentle yellow, frames burnished bright for the customer. Each prefers a different style.

This tired look was not always, however, the fashion. A London picture restorer expressed surprise at the change in fashion in his trade – though why, for heaven's sake, eludes me. Fashions in every other trade change. About fifteen years ago it seems that a dealer bought a picture of a dog – a tired picture way past its best.

'Brighten this up for me,' he had said.

'But this is way past its best,' said the restorer.

'Rubbish – a touch of red here, a bright blue curtain … Put some life into it.'

The painting came back to life and entered the market-place bright in its new coat, and was sold several times before the price began to lag a little. Fashion was changing. A dealer would by now be thinking that there was probably something under all that junk. This painting might be by a good hand, perhaps even a great one. The picture was returned to the restorer.

'Clean this off – let's go back to the original,' said the dealer.

'But there's only a fragment there.'

'Exactly – just what I want!'

So the painting of the dog became tasteful in muted colours, leaving much to the imagination, and is once again perambulating around the art market, its price restored as well!

HEARTBROKEN AND STOCKBROKEN

SOMETIMES you can be too careful. I recently returned from Italy with two rare and extremely interesting glasses made by Venini in the 1930s which I had nursed and protected from the ravages of Alitalia. I arrived at my shop and with the utmost of care unwrapped the first: there it was perfect – perfect even to its original label. Gently I placed it in the middle of my table and with caution unwrapped the next – again it was perfect, at least until it jumped from my hands falling directly on to the first bowl. Both were destroyed and I was left looking at a small heap of coloured glass. I am afraid this is an occupational hazard when you deal in glass.

One dealer of my acquaintance refused to allow his staff to touch glass after four o'clock in the afternoon on the basis that they were too tired by that time. This was really quite surprising as he seldom had a glass out of his hand after twelve in the morning, and, as far as I can remember, never dropped anything.

Breakages can sometimes be turned to a dealer's advantage – or so one Kensington dealer believed. He had just sold a majolica plate for a fabulous sum to a German client, taken his cheque and was passing the time of day while his female assistant wrapped the plate in the office, when he heard what can only be described as an ominous crunch. He quickly entered the office and there she stood, pieces of plate around her. 'Foolish child,' he said and she began to apologize. 'Wrap it up,' he said quickly, 'and give it to the customer.' He returned to the shop and continued his conversation with the German, during a long wait. The German was getting a little impatient when at last the girl appeared carrying the parcel. The dealer handed this over and somehow contrived as he opened the door that the German dropped the parcel. 'What a shame, probably broken,' he said, 'no chance of a refund, what a shame.' The German was speechless, the girl was somewhat agitated. 'Unpack the parcel, let's have a look,' hectored the dealer. To nobody's surprise the plate was broken into a dozen pieces. But, unfortunately, the girl had wrapped each broken piece individually.

Stories of broken glass abound. A tall flute, engraved with naked women by Maria Tesselschade Visscher, survived a trip across the Atlantic but was destroyed when it was being placed in its custom-made cabinet. Unfortunately the luckless keeper of glass in that museum did not realize that the shelves had been made too close to each other. As she took care the top got in all right the foot of the glass struck the lower shelf.

My favourite glass story is of the famous London dealer Christopher Sheppard, who, having travelled to Basle to buy a very rare glass, found himself a little short of money, so rode on the tram. Carefully he placed the glass on the seat beside him but within moments a large lady sat on it. Horrified he turned to protest: 'Ya,' she said, and 'Ya' was all he seemed to be able to get out of her. Later he got up and left the tram, the broken glass and the Swiss lady who seemed totally unaware of the mayhem she had wreaked.

Breakages, as I said before, are an occupational hazard of a dealer in glass. But imagine my surprise as I watched a customer examine a silver bowl – 3rd century BC. Greek and quite beautiful – the centre shaped like the fullest of breasts. Suddenly, exactly where the nipple had been, appeared his finger – right through the middle of my silver bowl – after the bowl had survived some 2300 years intact, which in itself, was quite an achievement.

Arms and the Man

When is a gun not a gun? When it is an oil pipeline, if the stories in the press about the Iraqi super gun are to be believed. In sheer size alone it seems to be without precedent, with its barrel, over a metre across, that bolts together in sections. This, however, is not the case. History has known one such gun. In the 19th century a large mortar was needed for the siege of Sebastopol and a civil engineer called Robert Mallet designed it. The gun was 11 feet long and weighed 42 tons; it fired a shell one yard in diameter weighing one and a quarter tons and holding 480 lbs of explosive. This, it was thought, would be powerful enough to penetrate the fortress the Russians had erected in the Crimea. The gun was so heavy that Mallet designed it in four or five pieces, none of which weighed more than 12 tons. When in position it was to be bolted together. All very similar to the Iraqi gun.

Mallet's first design was finished in 1854. Lord Palmerston ordered two of these guns at £4900 each from More and Company,

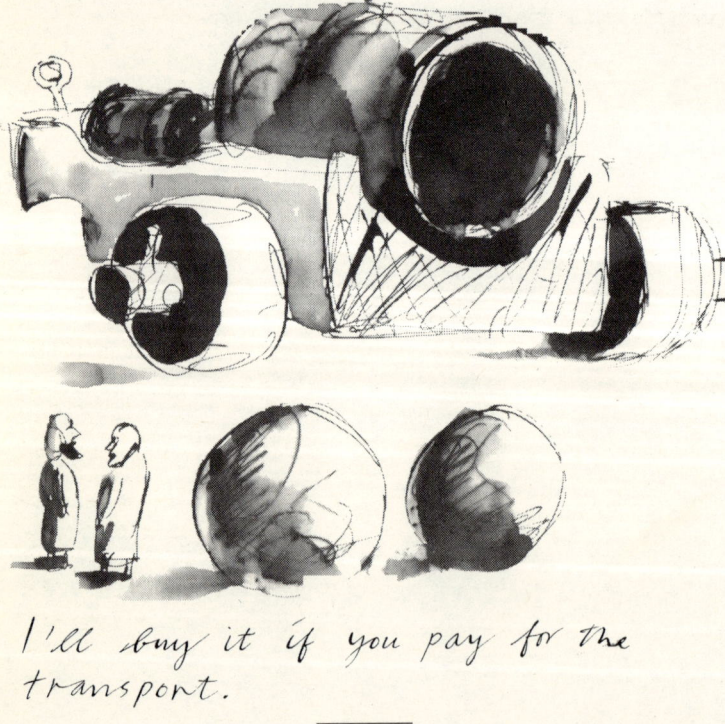

I'll buy it if you pay for the transport.

which were completed in 1857. When they were tested on Woolwich Marshes, a few shells were fired with success. The greatest range achieved was 2759 yards, but in the end, needless to say, the guns blew up and the venture was abandoned.

All my life, I have been interested in arms and armour. I think perhaps as a small boy that it was the romance of the knight in armour and the excitement of the Wild West that attracted my attention. Later, perhaps, it was the savage beauty of their purpose that I loved. In any event, I believe that these weapons of war, now obsolete and long retired, have a functional beauty – a sculptured quality. There are few shapes more elegant than the medieval sword, for instance. I have never really understood why it is that contemporary decorators will use a plaster bust reproduced for centuries rather than a morion (a 16th-century helmet) – an image of its own period and probably about the same price. I suppose it is mainly because most of them would not know a morion from a meat pie.

Guns are strange things to collect. But if you put at the back of your mind the purpose for which they are made, they do have a great beauty and, as antiques go, they are cheap.

In my youth, the dealers in arms and armour were a pretty strange lot. They all, however, had one thing in common: their kindness to me as a boy. Most are now long dead: the eccentric Mr Donald; Percy German, the butcher in Edgware Road who, when offered a collection of arms and armour – 20,000 items at one shilling each – bought it and changed professions to become one of the greatest dealers in that world; Robin Braid Taylor, always short of money, one of the most entertaining men I have ever met, always keen to buy, always on for a gamble; Fairclough, a jolly man like the proverbial farmer; Pip Roberts, an ex-waiter from the Savoy, whose shop in St Martin's Lane was a great centre for the buying and selling of almost anything but who had demon eye for a good gun; and Keith Neal, the grandest of them all, with one of the most remarkable collections in the world.

While still very young, I was invited fishing by an elderly friend of my father's and stayed the night at his house before setting out. That evening he gave a dinner party and, young as I was, I attended. I sat and listened to the talk, silent until the lady opposite me leant across the table and, in a voice to catch the conversation,

asked me what my hobbies were. I suppose that she expected the reply cricket, football, train-spotting. None of these things, I am afraid, interested me, so I replied arms and armour.

In shocked tones she repeated my words and added, 'When I think of boredom, armour comes immediately to mind. Armour is totally synonymous with boredom.'

I wish I could remember that lady's name, for I would like, now that time has passed and I am better able to debate, to talk to her about armour and the awful boredom of dinner parties before a day's fishing or shooting.

As the years have passed, armour has become a real fascination. The changes and development of it seem to parallel history, and its whole *raison d'être* the vagaries of the human psyche – all those protective instincts that forbid us from truly showing our emotions, that hold us from love and hate, that stiffen all our actions and constrict our lives so that we live bottled up, disguised and hidden from our fellows.

Value Beyond Measure

ALL collectors of course, are motivated by a passion. Having searched out objects of beauty, they are convinced and, indeed, sometimes convince their friends – of their deep love for the objects of their desire. However, it would not be unduly cynical to suggest that once the surface is scratched, a concern for price will be uncovered: for price and for value, for the two go hand in hand. No matter how much we might deceive ourselves, lurking in all of us is the question: 'If this cost me that, what can I sell it for?'

Consider *The Antiques Road Show*, that television programme whose panel of experts travels the country. The audience sits with its treasured possessions, finding it difficult to concentrate as some great guru describes in glowing terms the beauty of a 19th-century mahogany paintbox. They seem deaf, until the moment a price is estimated. 'Ah,' says the guru, 'how Arthur Negus would have loved this. Just look at the patina, the condition. A lovely little paint box. About £100 on a sunny day in a packed auction.' Just watch the disappointment.

Just observe how popular the show is, for people love to know the value of things. They might protest that it doesn't matter to them. That they will never sell it; that it was a gift from their aunt, and the value doesn't matter because they love it so much. Rubbish: deep down, it matters desperately.

The Western part of our world, at least, is obsessed with value. Our culture is about price and value, and in the end it is all in vain because objects do not change.

I have spoken before of the dealer in silver who, as a young man, watched his father. His father was very successful, and had much to teach. One day, the young man accompanied his father to Sotheby's, and watched him acquire, as the consequence of a succession of chances, a gold box at a bargain price. He took it back to his shop, and had not been there for more than a few minutes before a collector called on him, and saw the box. The collector studied it for 20 minutes, and the dealer waited with the patience of those very skilled in the art of dealing.

'How much?' inquired the collector; '£500,' replied the dealer.

'How much did you pay for it?' the collector asked; '£10,' said the dealer.

'I'll take it,' announced the collector.

'How very kind of you,' said the dealer.

'Not at all. It's the finest box I was ever offered.'

Unable to contain his curiosity, the dealer said: 'But the profit? You never objected to the profit.'

'No,' said the collector. 'I knew what you had paid. I just wondered whether you would tell me.'

Years later, when the young man had grown wise and, perhaps, a little cunning, having learned well from his father, he, too, sold beautiful boxes. And among his customers was a collector of gold boxes. Visiting the dealer one afternoon, the collector admired a gold box of blue enamel, set with diamonds.

'How much is this?' asked the collector; '£25,000,' he was told.

'And how much did you pay for it?' the collector asked, the dealer recalling his father's reply to the same question. Having admired both his father's style and the collector's reaction on that occasion, he ignored the fact that he had actually paid £22,500 for the box, which was worth all of £25,000 and maybe a few thousands more. He replied that he had paid £500 for it.

The collector looked at him with surprise, placed the box on the table, and wished him good afternoon. In imitating his distinguished father, the dealer had forfeited a handy profit. Thus, the last lesson he learned was that imitation is never a substitute for the real thing.

This was in the back of my mind only the other day at the Portobello Road market when I came across a Costa Rican mace-head – a figure carved in stone. It was offered to me by a mere lad for £70. That was trade price, I was told. I asked him if he would consider a lower sum.

'Not without asking my uncle,' he said, with uncompromising firmness.

'Discount for cash?' No, his uncle had given him instructions.

I thought about the mace-head for a few minutes because the price was cheap. It was far too cheap. Was the mace-head real? It looked real, but I wondered if this lad's uncle knew something I did not. The right price was about £1,500, so I walked away, but throughout the following week the thought of the mace-head worried me.

I sought out a dealer who knows about Costa Rican mace-heads and told him my story. 'The mace-head was a bargain,' he said.

I suggested that he accompany me the following day to Portobello Road and look at the piece.

'No need,' he replied, 'I know it well.'

'Know it well?' I said.

'I offered it to you six months ago for £2,000 and that's still the price.'

'Impossible. I was quoted £70.'

'Ah,' he replied, 'the lad made a mistake.'

Indeed he did. So did I.

Among the objects of my desire are snowdrops. Perfect white belles with drops of yellow or green, there are 200 varieties, maybe more. To most passers-by, snowdrops are the delicate white heads that push through the dead grass. They are the first movement in the garden, but no more or less than snowdrops. To the collector of snowdrops, however, a spot of green or a dash of yellow can mean the discovery of a whole new variety. Worthless really, one would suppose, except that, for me, it's priceless.

THE BRIC-À-BRAC OF LIFE

AT ten o'clock on the 16th of May 1990, Sotheby's auctioned the contents of my house, West Green, near Hartley Wintney in Hampshire. The accumulation of sixteen years of my life and a number of objects from the previous 25 years disappeared in almost a thousand lots and two full days of selling.

The 18th-century furniture of the Grand Saloon, the minerals of the mineral room were sold alongside the collection of over a hundred mocha ware mugs. These were mugs used in 19th-century pubs to drink beer, with white and blue bands of colour around them. On all of them the chocolate marks that give them their name, makes made by the craftsmen spitting their chewing tobacco at the damp glaze; strange marks the shape of trees. Wives used to say to each other, when their husbands returned late and a little less than sober, 'He was very tired last night– he's been lifting too many trees.'

The collection of garden implements from the 16th century to the modern, with its star attraction, a horse-drawn lawn mower, complete with leather coverings for the horse's feet – to protect the lawn – went. So too the shepherd's crooks in the hall, the stuffed birds in the master bathroom, all English birds. Collectively the bric-à-brac of my life, collected and hoarded. Each individual piece of great importance to the collector.

The mugs, the minerals, the garden implements, they went somehow with the house and I needed a new home with a different feel – harder, emptier, sharper. I am a nomad from a nomadic stock, setting little store in possessions. Anxious in their pursuit, casual in their disposal. I love many things, and hate quite as many. No work of art, however wonderful, is a substitute for its creator, nor of more consequence than the meanest man that would destroy it. Why sell all? To rid oneself of the chore of making a choice, to make a different style of life, to win the freedom to choose again.

The collections gone, dispersed, what is left? Snowdrops in the garden, over a hundred different varieties, a collection; hellebores, carpets of them in profusion, and roses, old garden roses, perhaps 400 varieties – the record of all these plants and their planting was lost in a fire. There are follies by Quinlan Terry, some built, some, as in all interesting gardens, only on paper and others only in the mind. And the garden itself, shaped and cared for by a human being, by chance called Mr Mann – sadly, now dead. A garden I hope in the spirit of the first owner of West Green, a certain General Hawley, a man who fixed the motto 'Do as you feel inclined' above his door.

Hawley used to visit his friend across the common, and one night, after they had dined well, Hawley picked up what he believed to be a lantern for his walk home in the dark. Out in the cold night air he was pursued by a terrible screaming; the faster he ran, the worse the screaming. Fearing the devil meant to collect his soul that night, he ran faster and ever faster – until he fell into a ditch where he stayed till morning. He awoke to find that he was clutching his friend's caged parrot. A garden with the ghost of Hawley's dog. A garden haunted, so word would have it, by Highland pipers coming to be revenged on Hawley, who led the cavalry at Culloden. They are as likely to be playing Hawley on, as opposing his charge, for more Scots fought on the side of the English than on the side of the Scots. There are even tales of buried treasure.

Many people have lunched there, drunk well I know, eaten well I hope, enjoyed West Green and its contents – some more than others. I remember a man who came to lunch; he held the party enchanted by his words, he made two jokes and all the room laughed and laughed. He made a third and there was silence. I mentioned this to him later, and far from embarrassment, he expressed delight. For he had, he said, an audience capable of discernment and it is the bad jokes that one should remember – failure is somehow funnier. How often it is that your true friends are not the most brilliant people that you meet and it is often a triviality which changes your life.

After Sotheby's knocked down the last lot, the marquee was gone, the garden swept, there stood only the obelisk that commemorates the life and work of Mr Mann, the gardener. His portrait in stone, a prize-winning goose between his legs, his hand on the obelisk with his back to the garden and all it might have been, thinking perhaps of what might be.

Do I regret leaving? I suppose that I do have a regret at leaving West Green. It is that I should have picked the snowdrops.

TWO

THE FRENCH CONNECTION

SHIRTLESS IN THE TUILERIES

As the French prepared for their holidays one year they were beset by lorry drivers who blocked all the motorways and farmers who set dead sheep alight – not to mention fishermen causing trouble in the Channel. Everyone in France seems to be in a bad humour these days. The taxi drivers evil-humoured as well; they have some private gripe against their government and are taking it out on the public.

Despite all this, France is still a wonderful place. I set off across the Place Vendôme in Paris to enjoy one of that city's great wonders – Charvet the shirt-makers, the most elegant and orderly of shops. I intended to place an order for some shirts and purchase a few silk handkerchiefs – pure luxury, what a way to start a day in Paris. The general ill humour of the French nation seemed to have struck this bastion of tradition too. They had a sale on, the lift was barricaded, and signs directed the crowds to the first floor, where the merchandise was heaped high enough to give each pile a certain instability. There were, however, no crowds, and few staff either for that matter. I found my way with some difficulty to the second floor, where they sell the shirts. This is a wonderful sight with bolts of cotton in a dozen quantities, and several hundred different patterns: stripes and checks, plain colours, and shades of each of these colours. There I found Joseph. Joseph comes from Egypt, and is a man of great charm and age. He was very helpful with the shirts. 'Show me your best quality of cotton if you please,' I asked. He did please, and produced a bolt of cotton of such quality that it was hard to tell from silk. 'Perhaps a dozen shirts,' I suggested, and then with some embarrassment I asked the price. Joseph, with equal embarrassment, told me. He gave me the strong impression that price is not an issue with the customers he serves. I wondered if he had indeed shown me silk, for all of the things that amazed me in that shop – fabrics, cuffs and collars in a multitude of shapes, intricate designs for embroidery – by far the most amazing was the price of those shirts. I left humiliated, muttering excuses over my shoulder.

As I recrossed the Place Vendôme I noticed office space to let. As I walked in the Faubourg St Honoré, there were empty shops. The recession seemed to be here as well. Nevertheless Paris is still a city of wonders and one is the Louvre and the Tuileries gardens. Building goes on apace; I M Pei still works away, though underground, doubling the exhibition space of that great museum.

Who needs more shirts anyway?

Thank goodness no more pyramids pop up in courtyards – not at the moment anyway.

Work has started on the gardens, the Jeu de Paume is restored and open as a gallery again, the fenced-off lawns are green once more. Maillol's plump girls are now displayed on their pedestals surrounded by grass. The trees are still unruly, however, the avenues of pleached chestnuts and plane trees no longer strictly pruned. Some trees have died and others have been allowed to grow too large, breaking a line that should have been as regimented as Napoleon's old guard; the gravel, what is left of it, is dusty, the parterres gone. Still waiting for children are the entertainments: the Punch and Judy show fast becoming derelict; the children's ponies standing bored and old, waiting for their small riders.

The tide of change is, however, sweeping down from the Louvre and will affect a secret garden in the most public of places – secret from all except those who walk on the embankment that borders the Seine. They can look down on to this patch of grass where tramps take their lunch, hidden by the builders' huts and tall shrubbery where convolvulus grows thick. An empty pond fills with their rubbish. In a few weeks, all this will be gone, the garden restored with swirling flower hedges and gravel paths, no accidents of nature allowed. Parterres and paths are beginning to materialize, lawns are laid and watered. Earth-movers move earth, plantsmen plant plants. Gravel is spread, the assorted stone sculptures that arrived at different periods in these gardens are now all imprisoned in a wire compound, waiting for masons to restore them and their bases – the bases lined by size, the figures caged in the solitary confinement of rough wooden crates. I stood watching all this activity lost in admiration for the French and their civic responsibility, never wondering how it was allowed to get into this state in the first place, forgetting that they forgot to do it all before.

WALLS HUNG WITH MONEY

FIAC (*Foire Internationale d'Art Contemporain*) '88 at the Grand Palais in Paris was the largest ever gathering of people and paintings in one place. (At least, that's how it felt.) The walls hung heavily with money. The packed crowd was thick with art groupies. 'Finger snacks' lasted only moments; wine was served in Perspex glasses and lasted a little longer. Gossip, heat, gossip, and noise.

The next day it was possible to appreciate the cool elegance of the stands. Nicholas Treadwell displayed his usual unusual taste – figurative and bizarre – out of the mainstream of painting. Gallery Hass showed a tribute to Lipchitz. Gallery le Bon hung Dubuffet's red, blue and white paintings (dismissed at the time, but each year seeming more beautiful); the Gallery Maecht about 60 or 70 small Calders worth £40,000 to £100,000 each.

There were stands for unknown artists, most of whom, I suspect, will remain unknown. The usual clutch of fashionable painters – Cucci, Paladino – sold large pictures for similarly large prices.

One stand had a selection of photographs by Robert Maplethorpe. Quite remarkable, but then the whole fair is remarkable. One year, Giscard d'Estaing performed the opening ceremony. When he was shown the stand of Sydney Janis from New York the president was amazed there were 30 important Mondrians. 'What a compliment to France!' he observed.

'Just old stock,' Janis replied, 'that I couldn't sell in New York.'

The prize for sheer quality this year went to Waddington Galleries. (I say this even though I am director of the firm.) On one wall were a Leger and two Picassos. A man would be considered a leading collector if he owned nothing else. One Picasso from the 1950s, *The Girl in the Red Dress*, is a pearl of great price: in other words, sell all and buy this if you possibly can.

A week's hard trading followed the opening weekend, and I suspect that towards the end of it much of the business was generated out of boredom and between exhibitors. They shouldn't have bothered. Outside, Paris was perfect, carpeted in golden leaves and glowing in the weaker sunlight of autumn.

Across the Seine, there are tall narrow buildings with top-floor flats with wonderful views over Paris. It was in one of these that a well-known dealer from London arrived on a similar autumn morning to deliver a large baroque figure. He was younger at the time and admits that the figure was monumental in scale and ugliness. He had bought it for a few pounds and it had lingered in his shop until *a Grand Parisien* asked him how much. The dealer, who loved a joke, said £5,000.

'Bring it to my apartment in Paris next Friday at midday, and I will pay you then,' the Frenchman said.

That is how the London dealer found himself carrying an enormous lump of wood up five flights of stairs. He rang the bell, and the door was opened by the *Grand Parisien* who, saying that he was in a hurry, handed over the cheque. The dealer was hurried out as well, but there was long enough to see that the apartment was stunning. The cheque looked nice too: a bearer cheque drawn on Rothschild's Champs Elysée branch.

The dealer was in a fine humour when he met a friend for lunch at the Petit Zinc. A simple bottle of Beaune became two. Two bottles became three, and when Rothschild's closed for the day, they were still talking about fine Burgundy. Indeed, they drank a great deal more of it during the weekend. On Monday morning, tired but happy, they presented the cheque at Rothschild's, where they were treated with great respect and asked to wait in a small room. The man who came to speak to them was not one of Rothschild's managers. He was however, a gendarme who announced that the cheque was stolen. Protesting their innocence, they were allowed to leave. Back at the fine apartment across the Seine, they found the *Grand Parisien* had gone, taking the baroque figure with him. The real occupant was not at all amused and they returned to London, sadder and wiser.

The dealer prospered and seven years later had a larger stock in a bigger shop. And one day the same *Grand Parisien* walked in and, pointing to another large ugly baroque figure, asked the price. Once again the dealer asked for £5,000, and the *Parisien* agreed, but on this occasion he produced two 18th-century Venetian silver-gilt figures of saints – rare and quite beautiful. Better still, they were offered in payment. The cheque may have been a fake, but the saints were real and worth much more than £5,000.

This time the *Parisien* took his purchase with him, and the dealer took his friend for lunch at the Connaught. When he returned to the shop, there was no sign of the silver saints. He assumed his girl must have put them away, but when he inquired, she said she hadn't. When questioned about the figures, she answered that the *Parisien* had taken them away when he came back for his umbrella. After all, as he said, they were his. Which just goes to show that lightning does strike twice in the same place.

Incidentally, the *Grand Parisien* comes from South America. Even his identity is a fraud.

ILLUSIONS OF GRANDEUR

ANYONE who has not noticed the boom in the art market should have been at Christie's sale of modern trains and other toys. They came from the Coluzzi collection and were beautiful indeed. Count Antonio Coluzzi spent his adult life collecting toys, and these are some of the prices:

Lot 737, a clockwork train set, circa 1882, £110,000. Lot 775, a steam engine, circa 1912, repainted and restored, £27,000.

This is fantasy, surely; it is difficult to know whether such things are art or memories, or what is the logic that persuades grown men to collect toys. (But if it depended on logic, who would collect at all?)

Lot 377, a liner constructed of tin in 1909, fetched £30,000, far more than you would have to pay for an illuminated page from a medieval manuscript. I suppose you can play with a tin liner in the bath, whereas a medieval miniature would become soggy and the paint would come off.

The only sense I can make of the sale is that you should never throw anything away, because you can never know who will want to collect it. All this demonstrates my contention that 'things' are not as they seem, which is one reason why series collecting is so absorbing.

Consider the case of the French jeweller who sold a single pearl of great beauty. The client told the jeweller that if he could find another just like it, to make a pair, it would be wonderful.

Impossible to match such a pearl, the jeweller said. In any case, a pair would be worth maybe 10 times as much as the single one. They would be worth it, the client said, and promised that if the jeweller should ever find a second pearl, he would pay at least four times as much as he had paid for the first one.

The jeweller had been serious in saying that it would be impossible to match the pearl, but collecting is an unpredictable business, and within a few months he found a second pearl that was in a different setting. He bargained long and hard for it, but the price he eventually paid was still twice as much as he had sold the first pearl for, and there was a small charge for changing the setting so that it matched the first perfectly. The jeweller wrote to his client announcing the acquisition and offering the pearl at the agreed price of four times the cost of the first one – plus, of course, the charge for the setting.

Weeks went by, and no reply. Eventually the jeweller met the dealer who had sold him the second pearl. 'Just as a matter of curiosity,' he said, 'whom did you buy the pearl from?'

'A very pleasant man,' the dealer replied, 'who told me that he had bought it for his wife. But she lost interest in it when she learned that she would never get the pair to it.' The French jeweller was mortified. He was one of the most experienced men in the trade, but was unable to tell that the pearl was what it was, and not what it was not.

There is another story of mortification among the French, concerning a young painter whose talent, though small, was just large enough to attract the attention of Renoir. The young painter had a rich, elderly relative who offered quite a large fee and suggested that he might paint a landscape, with two figures, girls perhaps.

The young painter was honoured by the commission and pleased by the thought of the fee, but after a few weeks the picture was in the doldrums. He had already reworked one part of it, but it lacked energy. Renoir took a brush and with a few strokes changed the reworked part of the picture. Impressed by what he saw, the master spent the rest of the afternoon completing that whole section of the canvas.

That evening, the young painter wrote to his patron that the painting was ready for collection. The relative, however, was pleased by only part of what he saw. That, he said, had the feel of a master. The rest was ungainly and crude. The relative asked him to repaint that part and said he would return in two weeks.

Disappointed at not getting the fee at once, the young painter set to work to repaint his part in the style of Renoir. But when his patron returned, he said he hated it.

'It is a pastiche,' he said, 'a pastiche of the great Renoir.'

The young painter was furious, not as you might imagine, with his patron, but with Renoir who, he felt, had lost him the sale.

He was wrong. His fury was without justification. His sad predicament was just one of those things.

JUDGEMENT OF PARIS

My old house, West Green, has returned to the National Trust, and Sotheby's cleared the premises. Only a handful of lonely lots remain – objects before their time or too long after it.

Free at weekends to travel, I can now look at places, their objects, and their character. Unencumbered. I have decided to become a tourist. A tourist is a traveller without purpose, who goes to see only the most obvious of sights. These, incidentally, are often the best and therefore lost to those of us who believe we are somehow grander. A collector of the truly wonderful would find it hard, after all, to ignore the Tower of London, the Empire State Building, Saint Paul's Cathedral or, for that matter, any of the world's great cathedrals, both ancient and modern. Each is a masterpiece of its own period.

So I travelled to Paris, visited Nôtre Dame and Sacré Coeur in a morning, and had lunch at the Tour d'Argent, instead of the smart little place where only the French go, which has become so insufferably boring. I like the Tour d'Argent. I like the food, I like the view, I like the Americans and I like listening to their conversation. They fascinate me beyond belief. Gems like 'I have a shower in the States, it has seven jets of water and they all hit the spine' abound. The reply is lost in the arrival of the pressed duck – the 737,579th duck that the restaurant has served – they only started to count in 1890.

I think it must have been lunch that slowed my pace. My new-found enthusiasm for the obvious slacking, I set out for the Musée de Cluny, the home of much medieval beauty, a museum of incredible charm.

Its collection spans 400 years – easy to cope with in an afternoon – and once seen it is always returned to. Housed in a 15th-century château, the collection ranges from belt buckles to sculpture. One room contains a set of tapestries depicting the legend of the unicorn and an ancient narwhal tusk, while pilgrim's badges vie with the grandest gothic chest, armour with candelabra. There are tombs and capitals, fragments and masterpieces, wood and stone carved in the High Gothic style, and a treasury filled with both Christian and barbarian gold. A newly covered courtyard is home to an array of sculpted heads and bodies (unfortunately not matching) and, in the middle, there is the most ravishing Gothic statue of a young man. Adam perhaps, hiding behind a heavily-pruned fig tree – French art at its very best.

No one can say that the French do not promote their heritage, for they promote it brilliantly. They have no hesitation either in mixing the new and the old – the contemporary sculpture in the Palais Royale is just one example of their architectural courage. Another, the new additions to the Louvre. What on earth would Prince Charles say to a glass pyramid in the forecourt of Buckingham Palace? Rather less, I suppose, if we were a republic.

The city is changing. In my youth, the French would never have painted a building. Now there is barely a public building that has not had half a ton of gold slapped on it. Red buildings, blue buildings, buildings of pipes and crazy Meccano sets, all jostle and compete with their neighbours – French architects with British and American.

Paris races to become fresher, newer, faster, trendier – the centre of artistic Europe and thereafter the cultural centre of the world. This is the French dream. They may well achieve it while we dawdle, arguing the toss between the past and the future. Eventually, if we as a nation stand still, build no brave new buildings and offend nobody, we will leave a gap in our heritage that our heirs will call the new dark age.

Paris, however, for all its beauty, is a cold city, populated by cold people who become familiar only in the sense of recognition, friendly but never friends; a formal city of formal people, entertaining in restaurants but never at the kitchen table. The city is sharper, new, its well-rounded edges have been honed, it is also harder. An American once said to me, 'Paris is a new pair of shoes, shiny and smart, but uncomfortable. London is an old pair, full of cracks, but my goodness they fit well and I would never throw them away.'

On for tea at the Ritz, one of Paris's oldest hotels, that sets a standard in hotel-keeping seldom observed in this age of worldwide chains. In the Franco-Prussian War, a careful owner, fearful of imminent invasion, bricked up the cellar, leaving a much smaller cellar in front. This space was filled with cheaper wines. At the time of the World War, the then proprietors did the same again. Only in 1970, after the brothers Al Fayed bought the hotel and decided to turn the basement into the world's most luxurious health club, was it that, much to their surprise, they found not one but all three cellars. The delight of this discovery was as nothing to the marvel of finding the contents untouched and perfectly preserved for a hundred years. Maybe this is what is really behind the Parisian desire to clean the whole place up.

Not Taking the Mickey

THERE is a strong likelihood of Euro Disney closing – its fate hangs in the balance, the victim of a high stakes game of bluff between backers and banks. The public of Europe are mostly indifferent, while those charged with handling Europe's cultural heritage are often positively contemptuous of whether Euro Disney stays or goes.

Euro Disney is Europe's only great manifestation of the need for entertainment that has dominated the second half of the 20th century: the World's Fair of the late 1960s held in Brussels has gone, all that remains of the Festival of Britain is scattered around the museums of the world or lurking in the shops and stalls of Portobello Road. Governments put preservation orders on disused power stations. Euro Disney is however, likely to pass unmourned. There are clubs and journals that record the passing of the steam train, with museums set up to preserve the few remaining examples; collectors eagerly search for old fairground equipment and ephemera. Yet the greatest example of fairground art in Europe is likely to be broken up and distributed amongst the world's street markets, with only those who have lost money in the venture having any regret.

I hated the idea of Euro Disney; for years I resisted all attempts to lure me to its American cousins. Then a year or so ago I was overcome by curiosity and visited this vast fairground outside Paris. I loved it so much I returned almost immediately. Clustered around a mock medieval castle stolen from the pages of *Les Tres Riches Heures du Duc de Berry* is a vast collection of conflicting architectural styles and national cultures. A sure recipe for disaster you might imagine – I did; far from that, I spent a night and a day there filled with delight.

First I hurried to a Southern Railway Station, whose attendants were dressed from the last century. I was directed to it by a lady attired in what must surely have been an army surplus uniform from Custer's 7th Cavalry. I climbed aboard the train; 'clang clang' went the bell, stirring music played and we headed into a tunnel – lightening flashed, stuffed animals stood in stuffed landscapes – of course I was right about how banal this all was. As we drew away from the tunnel Paris was gone. France was gone – we were in the American rockies. I knew because I travelled through them on a train some years ago. Below us was a lake with a paddlesteamer, beyond a township. The realism was staggering – I travelled through centuries on that train, and did not doubt any of it: I was terrified by the pirates of the Caribbean, lulled into a sensation of exuberant well-being by 'it's a small world'. I enjoyed it so much I went around the circuit three times.

I then lunched in the Key West Seafood Restaurant where the food and service were indistinguishable from America. I banged on the table with the wooden hammer for cracking crab claws – a tradition from the original restaurant at Key West: every time a fishing boat comes in a bell is rung, and every time that bell is rung all the customers hammer furiously – a quaint but contagious habit. Before long I was convinced that fishing boats were returning by the dozen across the plains of Northern France. Euro Disney is not deceptive but it does seduce you into self-deception. Disney only hints at what might be; it is your own imagination that fills in the gaps and extends these fantasies. Euro Disney shows those who believe that they have no imagination the possibilities of their own minds. I wandered past stores selling Disney in every shape and form. I stood and watched Disney's characters – many of the great images of the 20th century – cavort and play; all the while the music nudged my subconscious and I felt happy. I ate my dinner in a Western saloon, I slept in an hotel from New Mexico.

The next day I toured Euro Disney with a critical eye – surely the architecture was pure pastiche? Not at all. At first glance it seemed to come from the past; in fact it comes from the future, using the ethnic traditions of America as a starting-point. One thing was clear, the quality of the place, whether the landscaping or the building, the merchandise or the costumes – all were of the highest quality. The architectural detailing is magnificent, the imagination of its designers incredible. Should Euro Disney be closed and dismembered, within a hundred years some enterprising museum director will be raising money to buy bits of Disney Land in America and transport it to Europe just as the Americans transported our medieval architecture. This museum director will point out to those from whom he seeks his funds that Europe has no record of one of the world's greatest social phenomena. A fantasy built on an age of leisure.

THREE

ITALIAN MASTERPIECES

ECHOES IN THE MEMORY

WHEN I was 12 I met a boy who announced that he had visited 23 countries. This made my collection of coloured pebbles, a Japanese sword, Arab dagger and a bottled snake appear dull. Since then I have met collectors of jokes, of plays and operas and of sunsets. Much later I realized that at the age of 12 I had already met one of the most sophisticated of collectors. My contemporary collected experiences, and I have emulated him by collecting countries myself. Indeed, in the case of Australia I collect nothing less than a continent.

Italy is the prize in my collection of countries and I believe, contrary to the passionate advocates of either Florence or Venice, that Rome is the most delightful item in it; especially the squares.

There is the Piazza del Popolo, the square of the people, which has been seized upon by the municipal authority as a site for a car park and is therefore the square of the traffic. Yet it offers plenty to see from the cafés and restaurants that surround it, overlooked by the hills on two sides that make it resemble an amphitheatre. There is a fine Egyptian obelisk, but it is most remarkable for its twin churches, and when I sat in the square last I observed the celebration of twin weddings. The two brides arrived in two Mercedes limousines in what looked for all the world like similar dresses to be greeted by similar relatives.

The duplication was so striking that the arrival of one detracted from the appearance of the other, so, following a short conference, one bride was driven away to allow the first bride to make an entrance, before returning shortly after to make her own. Even in a square that does not rank highly for a collector of squares, there was an experience to delight a collector of experiences.

In the Piazza Navona, most of the traffic had been expelled and it is truly a square of the people. At one end is a strange, sinister mansion once used by the Gestapo, and condemned seemingly to sit dark and silent, treated with stubborn neglect. In stark contrast, at the other end of the square is a large toy shop. At first, this looks like a children's toy shop, except that there are no small toys, only large furry animals, not large toy animals either, but full size, like the eight-foot polar bear, the 10-foot crocodile, and the life-size pandas, zebras, leopards, tigers and kangaroos. The shop is an exotic zoo, or a toy shop for adults.

There are other rivalries in the Piazza Navona. At the centre of one side is the church by Borromini. Opposite is the fountain by his enemy Bernini, surmounted by an Egyptian obelisk held in place by four sea gods. They hold their hands over their eyes and turn their heads in horror away from the Borromini church – surely the most lasting and telling criticism ever made of an architect. Borromini responded by placing a lady on the roof of his church, her hands raised in admiration of his own creation. (The rivalries even extend to the quality of the ice creams in the Café de Colombo and the Café Tre Sealini. The Café Tre Sealini produces an ice-cream to beat all others – a chocolate truffle ice-cream. Break it open to find a collection in itself; nuts and segments of crystallized fruit.)

While in Italy, no collector ought to miss Urbino. The town itself is like any other Umbrian town, but the Ducal Palace is a masterpiece. It was built by Federigo, Duke of Montefeltro, and its courtyard and rooms strike exactly the right balance between simplicity and grandeur. With its parquet floors and plastered cornices, it is undoubtedly the superior of any other palace in Italy, perhaps the world.

The contents are not numerous but they are of the highest quality and it is possible to see four paintings that are not only among the greatest ever, but among the most interesting. *The Mute* by Raphael; *The Dream of Saint Jerome* (formerly wrongly titled as *The Flagellation of Christ*) of Piero della Francesca; Uccello's *Desecration of the Host*, a masterpiece of perspective.

The fourth is a work by an unknown painter of a town. It is no

It's
sure
Ducal

yep

ordinary town but a town as perceived by Renaissance man. I feel sure that Prince Charles would approve. It is classical and perfectly proportioned, but it is a town without people, flawless, empty and dull, not at all like the Piazza Navona or the Piazza del Popolo. This ideal town is without hope.

Whatever the aesthetes may think, architecture must be the servant of man, there for his pleasure, and if beauty suffers in that cause, then that is the fate of the aesthetes. The wonder of the Ducal Palace in Urbino is that it fills both roles, for it is full of beauty, and hope, and, on the day I was there recently, it was full of people too.

It is odd, but the collector of countries neither trades nor swaps, sells nor speculates. He might be the greatest collector of all, yet he owns nothing, except, of course, an enviable shelf of guidebooks.

BOLOGNESE RESOURCE

BOLOGNAISE sauce is served with spaghetti the world over, and wherever we find it outside of Italy it is one of the most repellant forms of food. The advance guard of Italian cooking, it has become universally used and abused. All this is strange since Bologna is the Mecca of food in Italy and the sauce that bears its name is, when served in its home town, pure magic. The cuisine of Bologna is the best in Italy – Italians say the best cuisine in the world, and there are good grounds for this claim. The Bolognese take food, and all things connected with it, seriously.

Bologna is a serious place. A red city. It has red painted buildings and, for that matter, is the heartland of the Communist Party in Italy. One of the few places left in the world where a genuine Marxist can still be found. The headquarters of the resistance to the recent change of name by the Communist Party of Italy. Communists they were and, despite the changes in Eastern Europe, Communists they wish to stay.

This must be something to do with the food, for in Bologna there are streets filled with food shops: fishmongers, greengrocers, butchers; and what is noticeable about these shops is the quality of the produce. Not in one shop, but dozens of them. Among the most remarkable is A F Tamburini, where there are heaps of cheeses and rows of cooked meats – amongst them a dish of pork crackling fried beyond recognition and with a taste so good that it is beyond description. Dishes of olives, perfect in size and shape. Piles of different sausages, wines and breads.

Travellers go to Rome and one hears them talk of Florence and Venice, but while the cognoscenti visit Lucca and Urbino, Bologna has an industrial ring about its name that turns the visitor away. Bologna, nevertheless, is a town of beauty with its arcaded streets – not just the main thoroughfares, but the lanes as well.

Bologna's medieval museum, for me, is a perfect one. Small enough so that the whole of it can be seen in less than an hour, it has the most comfortable seats I have ever found in any museum. I have never approved of people who sit on benches and stare at objects for hours on end, but in here I would happily sink into one of the sofas that are in every gallery and rest in comfort surrounded by objects of beauty, thinking my own thoughts and looking at more of these. The museum begins with a cabinet of curiosities. A small cabinet, but a real one, complete with objects from exotic lands collected in the 16th century, including a unicorn's horn and a chastity belt, without which no cabinet would be complete. The museum also has a small group of stone crosses from the 12th century, crosses mounted on the remains of Byzantine columns. They used to be positioned at the intersections of all roads in the district, but Napoleon when he came to Bologna undertook a plan of urban redevelopment and the crosses were nearly all destroyed. The remaining examples (only 10 or so) are strange and wonderful.

Bologna has its share of grand churches and Renaissance buildings. However, it is not a beautiful town in the sense that Venice is a beautiful town. It is a workmanlike town where the people work hard. The people seem dull by comparison with those in Milan, but they do have heart and soul. In the main square there is a fountain with a figure of Neptune, who presides over four putti playing above the heads of mermaids, whose breasts liberally distribute water. This fountain by Giambologna was made in 1556, and has recently been restored. The restoration took place in a large wooden hut nearby. This hut, smelling inside like a Scandinavian sauna, was built for the occasion and named Neptune's House and is now used for the restoration of other of the town's monuments. The public are admitted and they can walk along galleries at different heights to watch conservators at work with hoses and scalpels. All this to sympathetic music. As you leave, it is suggested with the utmost of tact that you might like to contribute to the activities of these conservators. There is, in my view, no better way to raise money for these purposes than to show the public how it is spent. There is nothing that the public enjoys more than to be admitted, if only for a few moments, behind the scenes. Many of our great museums, always in search of funds, might do well to study the example of the town council of Bologna. The Bolognese are a polite and precise people. They think about projects before they undertake them and they do not encourage waste. In the cafés around this town when you buy a cup of coffee you are given water as well, but here only in a small glass.

There is wealth in Bologna, real wealth – not just a few rich people. A large part of the population are wealthy and they know why, for they work extremely hard and carry a large part of Italy on their backs.

A Cut Above in Milan

MILAN is not one of the world's most beautiful cities. The Milanese have not had, over the centuries, a great interest in architecture in the same way that the Florentines or, for that matter, the Romans have had, rather the reverse. In fact, it took them over 400 years to complete their cathedral. If it had not been for Napoleon who said 'For the sake of God, finish this work now,' I imagine they would still be building it. Milan however, has grown its own beauty, a beauty of spirit, a beauty of enterprise, a beauty that comes from the natural exuberance of the Milanese. You can see it in their great manes of hair, in the heavy gold jewellery and diamonds that they wear. Milan is, by and large, a city of wealthy people and they show it. While the women of the rest of the world are afraid to be seen in even the skins of rabbits, the Milanese wear sable at the first sign of a cold spell. They are unashamed in their pursuit of luxury, so their city has some of Italy's finest restaurants and certainly the world's finest grocer: Salumaio's. A shop of such beauty that it seems a crime to buy anything and to spoil the patterns: patterns of glazed meats, patterns of mushrooms, patterns of pastas – food that has been treated with as much artistic care as culinary. In the same streets, Via Napoleone, where you can find Salumaio's is the Café Cova, an old-fashioned teashop with straight-backed chairs, ancient waiters and bridge rolls filled with ham or egg. A strange survivor from past years packed, however, with the Milanese.

This is not a tourist city filled with bemused foreigners, it is a working city used to its limits by its citizens who revel in the wonder of their own town. In this age of tourists packaged here and packaged there, it is a phenomenon well worth observing. Milan must be one of the greatest shopping towns in the world: jewels, fashion, food and G. Lorenzi, the seller of knives. G. Lorenzi sells only the greatest of knives, not knives like the Swiss Army Penknife – a knife with a hundred uses and useful for none of them. This very name should give a hint of its value as a useful implement: the Swiss Army cannot have been in action for many centuries. The penknife, similarly, with its bright red colour, small white cross and multitude of blades, is only useful for small boys to show to their friends; under no circumstances would I use it for any serious purpose. Lorenzi's knives, on the other hand, are very serious, made by master cutlers, the doyens of their trade. Tommy Lee, Jim

Kelso, Howard Hitchmouth and Christian Wimpff. These men produce knives of great beauty, blades made from several hundred strips of metal pounded together, ivory carved handles, grips made from rare woods and semi-precious stone, steel engraved by the most talented of engravers. One knife by James A Schmidt of New York with a handle made from stag's horn carved with the face of a goblin, his eyes small opals, sells for £5000. Why not – that, after all, is only a fraction of the price of a ball gown by Valentino. Milan is that sort of city: steak knives by Deniq, £1,500 each – and the forks that go with them?

'Well,' said Mr Lorenzi, 'that's a problem. It's very hard to find a competent fork-maker today.' He had what seemed to be a perfectly good range of forks. 'Those forks – how could you use those forks with Mr Deniq's knives, the tines are square,' and sure enough they were.

'What on earth difference does that make,' I asked.

'The taste,' he replied. 'The taste of the meat. A square tine tears the meat, the right size of rounding just pierces the meat.'

How wonderful to find a man so steeped in his craft, but my general experience with sharp, round tines is that, although they pierce the meat well, they also tend to pierce the tongue.

Mr Lorenzi sells not only knives but also cigar boxes made just to your specification, a range of strange pipes and unusual walking-sticks and then really useful items like a bonsai pruning set; twenty or so surgical-like instruments in a smart leather roll; and, the most exotic of all, a strange contraption with an ashtray, a small clip and a rubber ball. Mr Lorenzi explained to me that you light your cigar, place it in the ashtray, put the still burning match in the clip and press the ball to expel the air from inside it – puff, the match is out. I suppose that this machine is for a man with extremely bad breath. A city of shops that sell pointless luxuries?

The Milanese work hard – and as for luxury, what we call luxury is never pointless, for the providing of luxury enriches the lives of all that it touches. Like it or hate it, approve or disapprove, luxury is that strange fantasy without which the world would be an empty place.

Paradise in Padua

Twenty-five years ago I visited Padua for the first time. It was the end of September and the weather was still warm, but there was a mist that hung about the city that day, a feel of winter in the air. I walked down a cobbled street. The leaves had just begun to drop from the willow trees that edge an adjacent canal, and ahead of me stood the gate piers of l'Orto Botanico dell'Università di Padova – the Botanical Gardens of the University of Padua – the oldest botanical gardens in the world, founded in 1545.

I have often returned to Padua, a fine city well worth the trouble of revisiting, but why should my memory hold so exactly the details of that first visit? It was the Botanical Gardens – never for me have they looked more beautiful: the high gate piers, one pair on each of the four sides of this garden, with large urns atop them, urns grotesquely disproportionate to the columns, urns with wrought-iron leaves growing in them; wrought-iron gates between the piers. The gardens are encircled by a high wall; inside this wall is a magic world – flowerbeds laid out in symmetrical patterns, small boxes edged in stone, each one with a different plant growing in it. The whole of this enclosed garden is not more than a hundred paces in diameter. There are beds around the inside edge of the wall and then a circular path – inside which are four squares with radiating beds, and fountains at the squares' centres. The whole garden is dissected by a path running from gateway to gateway and at the point where these paths join there is a rondel, again with a fountain. The plants? On that day they had all been cut down; in each of the stone compartments stood only stalks cut off an inch or two above the ground, and a label in iron to describe what had flowered there the season before.

The mist, the stone, the gravel of the paths, the bare stalks and the fountains that did not run. I have often returned to that garden. I have seen it flower and I have seen it coming into flower. I have seen it become more derelict and I have seen it the subject of a considerable amount of attention. The urns have fallen from the gate piers on which they sat; for some years they just lay there until a tidy-minded keeper put them together and now they stand at the feet of their columns.

The fate of this garden has always been one of ups and downs. Seven years after its founding there were 1500 species of plants, some of which, first introduced to Europe in these gardens, have now become common; for instance the potato in 1590; lilac in 1565; rhubarb in 1612; the sunflower in 1563; and what I suppose was a great novelty in 1642 but has since become the gardening equivalent of a cliché – *Parthenocissus quinquefolia* or Virginia creeper.

It was Francesco Bonafede who persuaded the Senate of the Venetian Republic to set up this garden, arguing that you cannot teach in the abstract alone, and that it was important for the students of medicine to see the plants from which cures they could prescribe came. The gardens have remained virtually untouched since that day. Their contents, however, have had good times and bad. By 1752 there were 3500 species, a hundred years later 16,000 species, but by 1945 only 3800. And then, after the war, came good times and the number of different species held by the gardens had increased to 6000 by 1983.

The enclosed gardens are surrounded by an arboretum of about two acres. The trees here are not particularly exciting, though several have been planted on special occasions or by special people; one, a chestnut tree planted by the founder, unfortunately looks as though it has not much longer in this world. In an attempt, I suppose, to add to the attraction of this garden, small areas have been set aside for rock plants and cacti. Here, as almost everywhere else, it becomes clear that less is better than more – this garden will benefit only from putting a stop to improvements. Beyond the garden walls rise the towers and domes of the Church of San Antonio – a view that has remained unchanged for centuries.

My most recent visit to the gardens was last August. I was very taken with the small area devoted to aquatic plants: the same geometric beds edged in stone, but with water in them instead of soil. Two nymphaea took my fancy: *Nymphaea victoria*, the giant waterlily named after Queen Victoria, its leaves several feet across, famous from the engraving of the specimen at Kew where a small child is shown standing on a leaf; and a nymphaea I had not seen before: *Nymphaea euryale* – another large-leafed waterlily, its leaves like the skin of the crocodiles that I am certain lurk beneath it in its native waters. Beside these two exotic waterlilies is a tank with lotus plants in it: *Nelumbo speciosa* 'Williol' was then in full flower, which did not surprise me in northern Italy, for it is quite possible to grow and flower the lotus plant in the open here.

Climbing around the urnless gate piers were two varieties of *Campsis*, both in bloom, one red, one orange. On one of these piers is fixed a notice in stone, erected when the gardens were founded. This notice says, roughly translated from the Italian, 'Do not knock on this door before ten o'clock in the morning or before Saint Mark's Day. Do not in any way damage the plants or stand on them, or you will be punished by a fine, imprisonment, and exile.' It seems that the Italians of the 16th century took their gardening rather seriously.

BARTERHOUSE OF PARMA

PROWLING through the pages of a magazine, I came across an announcement of the 12th annual *'Mercante in fiera'* to be held in Parma the following weekend. This great gathering of dealers in antiques and objects one day destined to be antiques boasted 600 exhibitors. The theme this year, for reasons that escape me entirely, was 'Return to the Future'. However, accompanying this announcement was a colour illustration of a most splendid jukebox. I had never been to Parma before, and my friends had told me that it was a fine town – the birthplace of Verdi they said.

They were right about Parma, it is indeed a fine town, even in Italy, a country stuffed with fine towns. Parma has good food and good buildings: its baptistry is perhaps the best Romanesque building in the whole of Italy; its cathedral dates from the 12th century. Hidden in a monolith of a building built in the 16th century to house soldiers, their supplies, and the men who administered the State, is the most wonderful court theatre. Destroyed during the war, the theatre has been faithfully rebuilt – if the guidebook had not confessed to this I would never have guessed. My friends were wrong in the matter of Verdi's birthplace, for he was born at Bossetta, a small town a few kilometres from Parma. However it is in Parma that Verdi is revered – his works are performed to perfection in Parma's Opera House – its audience perhaps the most knowledgeable about his work anywhere and so also the most critical.

The rain on the day I arrived in Parma came down continuously and as solidly as palings in a fence. I was soaked on my way from the taxi to the entrance of the *'Mercante in fiera'*, a dash of fifty yards. I then set out to walk around the great gathering of 'antique' dealers. I measured my morning's walk; it was slightly more than seven kilometres in total – the stalls check by jowl and piled high with goods. I do not know how many paintings, prints and objects were offered for sale there, but the number must have run to several million. I have spent most of my life visiting fairs and I have never seen the like. There were of course many stands that sold brown furniture, and even more of pictures of varying quality, but never before have I come across a man who deals exclusively in cookie jars. Some were in the shape of the characters from *The Muppet Show* and *Sesame Street*, some from the last century and even, I suppose, the century before – though these jars probably contained biscuits. My favourite was a monk whose head lifts off to allow you to get at the cookies. This monk had written across his chest in bold letters: 'Thou shalt not steal'.

I have come across dealers in gramophones before, but never dealers in scent bottles; I have seen second-hand sunglasses for sale – on occasion I have bought a particularly snazzy pair – but never before have I found a shop where they sell nothing but sunglasses; and so it went on all seven kilometres of my perambulation around the sheds that held this fair. I found four stalls that sold only second-hand telephones, stalls selling medals and stalls selling make-up, and unlike the dealers in tables and chairs of dubious age that purport to come from the 17th and 18th centuries these dealers were all doing splendid business.

What fascinated me was that even when they were not selling their scent bottles, make-up or second-hand telephones, these stalls were crowded with people looking at what they offered. The truth of the matter is that the urge to collect spreads far wider than is generally realized. The brown furniture and paintings judged useful by most people furnishing a home are not regarded as items they have any real desire to collect, it was the dealers selling fountain pens and watches who were doing the business. The market these days is in the second-hand. Strangely, I came across only one or two stalls offering second-hand clothes – I had expected rather more – but then America is the Mecca of second-hand clothes, and perhaps that fad has not yet reached Italy. One stall sold only black lace and jet jewellery; it was, I must say, quite beautiful.

This fair was the home of the specialist dealer and specialist collectors seemed to be there in profusion. The dealer in juke-boxes was the one who caught my fancy – including the juke-box whose picture had drawn me to Parma in the first place. I had an idea: I would own this wonderful machine with its flashing lights and stained-glass façade; I would fill it with recordings of Verdi's great arias, and at the insertion of a coin and the press of a button they would blast across my sitting room. 'How much is this machine?' I asked. 'Sixty million lire' came the reply. I protested at this, the dealer looked at me with contempt. 'It has all its original plastic,' he pointed out. Such are the antiques of the future.

THE BUYING GAME

ROME in the early summer is always warm, and often extremely hot. This was one of those hot days: the Spanish Steps were crowded with young tourists and the sellers of cheap paintings and grotesque caricatures of girlfriends and family, and among them was a new trade I had not seen on the steps before – men and women who braid coloured beads into the hair of other men and women. I scrambled through the seated ranks of buyers and vendors and those there to watch or just to rest. I clambered past the flower sellers at the foot of the steps, past the tourists who bathe their feet in the fountains, and out into the streets of Rome, into a world of squealing brakes and snorting scooters.

These are not the sort that as a young man I used to ride – decorous, upright Lambrettas or Vespas transported me. Rome used to be populated with them; young men at the handlebars with their girlfriends perched side-saddle behind, clinging to their male friends with more than the enthusiasm of companionship, for these young men and women risked their lives in the streets of Rome. Now the men drive a Piaggio, a Spacy, a City Express or a Suzuki. The women sit astride and it is the pedestrian who is at risk. One vehicle I came across rejoiced in the name of the Nippomoto Urban Kid – a truly remarkable means of transport. I wandered in the side streets – walking cautiously along the crowded pavements of Rome's main thoroughfares, always wary of those modern scooters and the midget motor cars that creep up on you, then knock you down. For Rome's traffic is a legend – almost stationary where it is supposed to flow, moving with the speed of summer lightning where no traffic is supposed to be, and all the while the day seemed to become hotter.

I headed towards a bar that I recalled in the Via Croce. I never knew its name. I did not need to – it was always there, a haven from summer heat, tourist crowds and the confusion of the abusive traffic. The bar in the Via Croce was no ordinary bar; it seemed caught in a time warp – cool and cavernous – and around its walls racks of the world's greatest wines. The bar was of faded mahogany trimmed with zinc; its till had a brass grille and an aged cashier – just as it should be – and there were small china trays of *ciccetti* (snacks) on the bar. Behind it were cold stone sinks filled with bottles of wine – wine of several dozen different vintages by as many and more different makers – which could be bought by the glass. A barman who possibly owned the bar would discuss the merits of the different vines as you drank – a man of intelligence who knew when to speak, who to speak to and who to leave to their thoughts. I walked through the door and the bar was gone, or rather it had changed so much that it was as if it had never existed.

In all undertakings that pull ahead of their fellows by showing a quality and care in how they conduct their affairs, who become yardsticks of which people say, 'I admire that', or 'I would love to own that', there comes a time when they should close. The bar on the Via Croce was like that. How much better if I had found in its place a shop selling shoes or cheap clothing – far better death than a humiliating decline. One of life's curious features is that those who buy a business, which they and many others have greatly admired, imagine the one thing that their new aquisition needs is changing. They then proceed to do just that, ruining what was in its way a masterpiece. These people have neither the originality nor the wit to spot which aspect of a business truly constitutes quality; they buy great names and strive to make them greater – in fact they destroy them utterly.

I once nearly fell into this trap. I owned a bookshop and desired to expand the business, so I sought to buy a fellow bookseller's business – Heywood Hill. I had long admired that bookshop, it was run in the way a bookshop should be run. I entered into negotiation and we arrived at a satisfactory price; the shareholder would sell, I would buy. However, I did not buy. I hesitated and then I drew back, for I knew that if I owned that business I would change it and to change it would be to ruin it. I stopped – for I liked it as it was.

There is a difference between being a customer and the role of a proprietor. The bookshop that I took pleasure in as a customer would become a millstone round my neck if I had responsibility for its management – happily Heywood Hill fell into the hands of a man who owned no other bookshops and has left it unchanged. I buy my books there and take pleasure from the fact that it exists much as I knew it. Those days were long ago now, and I have learnt that among life's myriad pleasures, the pleasure of ownership with all its responsibilities is the least of them.

ROMAN CARNIVAL

In Rome one month I took my own advice and queued on a Sunday morning to visit the exhibition of glass, now long disposed, from the time of the Caesars in the Campidoglio. To queue in the Campidoglio is no great hardship, and even if the wait had been twice as long, it would still have been worth every moment. The exhibition was stunning; there were almost 200 pieces of Roman glass drawn from the world's greatest museums. Four pieces stood out, each for a different reason.

The Portland vase was much smaller than one imagined, blue with figures in white relief, who are contemplating either life or each other. In any event, it is the most famous piece of glass in the world, much copied, especially by Wedgwood (the copy itself is now worth a great deal of money). Were it not safely housed in the British Museum, the Portland vase would give Van Gogh's *Sunflowers* a run for their money under the seductive hammer of Charlie Allsop at Christie's.

The next outstanding piece was a small bust of the Emperor Augustus. An inch or so high, it was green with a touch of red in the hair, not copied, but quite beautiful.

A much promoted *Coppa di Licurgo* was illustrated on the cover of the catalogue. This cup, about four inches high, was mounted in the 17th century with a silver gilt stem, foot and lip in green glass that changes to red. It is an extraordinary piece, with giants and satyrs, huntsmen and dogs, in high relief.

The last of the four, my favourite piece, was notable for its modesty compared with the flamboyance of the other three. It was a small millefiore bowl, almost four inches in diameter, with a tiny portrait set just off centre. The beauty of this bowl was not obvious, but it was worth all the rest put together.

Just walking round the exhibition was an illuminating experience, and now I know how a certain London jeweller felt when he visited Christie's to view a sale. He arrived to find a sale of antiquities about to start, and was taken with the ancient glass. That sale was 10 days before Christmas, so he bid for and bought a beautiful Roman millefiore bottle as a Christmas present for his wife. He cleared his lot and returned to his shop, where, distracted by a customer, he placed the glass on a table behind the door and thought no more of it. That same morning his wife was suffering after the Christmas rush in Harrods. After hours of indecision and being pushed here and there she found a pair of socks for him. Then, exhausted, she returned to the shop, and, given to a little drama, threw the door wide open.

'I'm exhausted,' she said.

'Oh my god,' he said.

'Is it that bad?'

'I think you have just broken something.'

Imagine how the jeweller felt next day when he read in *The Times* saleroom report that he had paid a world-record price for the millefiore bottle.

Leaving the exhibition, I came into the bright sunlight. It seemed to put another coat of shellac on the roofs of Rome, and standing in the Campidoglio, I understood that the greatest

Trajan must have loved it.

collection in the world was here before me. I do not mean paintings or sculpture. I do not mean great works of art. I mean Rome, the lazy ease of women with hair almost as long and languid as themselves, the noisy smell of the cars, the absolute vulgarity of Gucci's store, the crowd gossiping at the Café Greco.

The whole city is one sociable café in which to meet your friends to walk, to gossip, to argue, to debate, to move, to shout, to cry. The ringing of bells, the uncertainty of the museums. Will they really open? Is it worth waiting? The proliferation of gypsy beggars – there are more than half a million of them camped around the city – and the food. The food is a collection on its own: baskets of mushrooms in vegetable markets that block the most fashionable of streets.

Flower sellers and peasant pipers come dressed in goat skins from the hills for religious festivals. In the churches at Christmas there are baroque figures surrounding a crib that were made in the 17th and early 18th century; they are quite beautiful and much sought after. Occasionally they are found in salerooms. There are the palaces, *piazzi* and *campi*, obelisks and cobbles, unchanged over centuries. Because of an absence of planning, urban architecture mixes with industry, blocks of flats with horse paddocks and scrapyards.

In another part of the city, Mussolini's new Rome is clean, ordered, unfinished and somewhat frightening. Frighteningly similar to the architecture that Prince Charles would have us admire today. Then, in the centre of Rome, the building that the Romans call The Wedding Cake: the great memorial to Victor Emmanuel, first king of Italy, layer upon layer of white marble.

Rome is either the greatest collection or, alternatively, the greatest collector, for it has all the qualities of the collector, greed, energy, avarice, and most importantly an ability to justify excess. Rome has that sublime vulgarity and the collector needs to be ahead of his time. Like collectors, Rome is able to hide a masterpiece and display it when the time is right.

Whether it is the collector or the collection, Rome has for the past two millennia been an inspiration and the source of many of the objects that the greatest of collectors have wanted to collect. Collect it at once.

A Roamer in Verona

The rain had fallen for several days, hard rain. The cafés in the Piazza Brà were deserted – outside that is. The tables where tourists normally sat eating their ice-cream and drinking *tè freddo* made from peaches (popular in Verona's hot summer), stood in pools of water. The rain had washed the dirt of the tourist season off the pink marble pavement, revealing its true colour, and had polished the marble built into the walls of the great amphitheatre where, on summer evenings, opera is performed.

The productions are often gigantic. For *Aida* or *Turandot* the cast is sometimes over a thousand strong. The rains come in the summer as well, but the orchestra is quickly covered in plastic sheeting. The audience, wearing pack-away raincoats, leave the arena to sit in the bars until the downpour is over. The opera fans who visit Verona are a robust lot. I can recall a famous tenor being heckled unmercifully. He stood, during the last act of *Tosca*, on the battlements of Castel Sant' Angelo, the Roman castle where Cavaradossi is taken to be shot, and he sang. The evening breeze filled his shirt and it expanded like a tent. The same breeze shrank his voice, and as he sang 'for shame for shame' the audience, almost as one man, shouted back, 'what a shame he is flat, take him off'.

In winter the chairs are taken to store and the arena is bare, with just the remains of some set, no longer wanted, piled beneath an arch. The tourists gone, only the Veronese sit in the cafés; they read the papers, drink hot chocolate and eat brioche. Most of the trees in the piazza have lost their leaves, the water drips from the branches of the cedars, the weather is cold.

Verona is situated in the shade of the mountains. The summers are hot, very hot, with occasional storms, the winters cold and wet. The people – as with all northern Italians – work hard, and have over the last few years prospered, though the opera fans who come to the city in the summer are not the source of the city's wealth. The arena holds 26,000 people and a few more uncounted who climb in over the walls. The visitors are a bonus, filling hotels in the summer season when all right-minded Italians take their holidays. The city sits in an industrial area and industry is how it earns its living. The shops sell good clothes, particularly shoes – the whole place is filled with shoe shops – and china and glass of quality also seem to be popular. The Piazza delle Erbe, whose wonderful name conjures up stalls of country produce and the sweet smell of freshly picked herbs, is not so at all. Rather, stalls that sell large buns stuffed with roast pork or sausages, and all the smells that go with this trade. The Piazza is also a market for cheap clothes and small birds, of which there are too many to a cage – a study in cruelty, needless and wasteful. The shops of Verona have their own eccentricities. Shops specializing in umbrellas or hats are seen in many towns; shops that boast 70 varieties of tea, as one does in Verona, are not uncommon; but where other than in Verona will you find a shop that only sells toothbrushes? Toothbrushes of all shapes and sizes, brushes for a dozen or more different purposes, and the paste to go with them – small tubes of paste, flat tubes with just enough paste for one night, coloured brushes and paste to match.

In winter the river Adige which flows through the town is a cold green; in summer it looks no warmer. On one bank stands Castelvecchio (old castle), so called simply because at the end of the 14th century two new castles were built. Like other castles over the years, Castelvecchio was knocked about quite a bit. After the last war it was largely restored and used to house the city's collection of medieval paintings and sculpture. In the early 1960s the castle had the good luck to fall under the control of Carlo Scarpa, the architect commissioned to superintend its final restoration. This he completed in 1964, using the materials of the 20th century with great style – concrete with a planked surface and iron girders left exposed.

There is, in this building, no conflict between the old and new; thanks to the care with which he chose the scale of every beam or truss, the boldness of his materials allows no conflict with the work of a different age. Carlo Scarpa approached his task meticulously – every hinge, every lock is carefully considered; nothing is random, nothing left to chance. Carlo Scarpo designed a base for each piece of sculpture, the grandest being the platform on which the equestrian statue of Cangrande stands. The statue of Cangrande, a lord of Verona and the man who built the castle, dates from the early 14th century. He sits astride his horse, his great helmet hanging on his back, both man and beast wearing armour. The platform, a slab of rough-cast concrete, is cantilevered from a wall of the castle, high up so that Cangrande looks out over the river and at his great bridge that spans it. Above his head is a roof to protect this extraordinary work – arguably the world's greatest equestrian sculpture. Carlo Scarpa has done well by Cangrande and he has done well by Castelvecchio, for what was once a Renaissance castle housing a fine collection of art, is now turned into a masterpiece.

Pissoir Artist

It is not the change in the weather that heralds spring in Venice, rather the pack of motor boats that prowl the Grand Canal in the vicinity of the Palazzo Grassi. The reason for their presence at this time of year is the opening of the annual Palazzo Grassi blockbuster – this year the work of Marcel Duchamp. The cargo that the motor boats carry are guests on their way to the official opening. These boats push and shove to land their important passengers on the palazzo's private landing stage. Those less pushy or not so well practised in the art of shoving have to spend some time prowling that stretch of canal waiting their turn. In any country other than Italy, in any town other than Venice, the passengers would have been dropped at the *vaporetto* (water-bus) stop, a place from which it is just as convenient to enter the palazzo as it is by its own landing, but not here. This is the land of *bella figura* (good face), and it must be the official entrance with its line of civic officials doing the greeting or nothing. To enter the Palazzo Grassi from a bus stop would definitely be *brutta figura* (bad face), and such behaviour might take years to live down – indeed a man's social standing could be entirely destroyed by how he arrived at an exhibition of the work of Marcel Duchamp.

There is an extraordinary irony about all this, for Duchamp was tackling exactly this aspect of life when he first exhibited a urinal. I chose it therefore it is art, he said, – or words to that effect. The argument has raged ever since, but sure enough, Duchamp's urinal is hung in the Palazzo Grassi – not at eye-level as a picture is hung, not on a pedestal on the ground as a sculpture is shown; no, the lavatory basin is hung about right for a full-grown man – too high for small boys. The day I went to the show there was a group of large men behaving like small boys around that urinal. I was left wondering whether Duchamp always intended the audience that looked at the piece to be the work of art rather than the pan itself.

Duchamp is perhaps best known for the objects he used to provoke: the bottle rack; a box full of measuring implements; a stool with a bicycle wheel mounted on the top of it. (I suppose it may have been used in a garage to ease the repair of punctured tyres.) Chosen by Duchamp, all these objects provoked an argument about the nature of art. Then there are the casts of intimate parts of the human anatomy and the defacing of

Leonardo's *Mona Lisa* – she looks very well in a moustache painted by Duchamp. These are works all about Duchamp the thinker. The exhibition is light on the work of Duchamp the painter, inevitably I suppose, for his paintings of real consequence came only during a very few years when he worked in a style that was truly his own.

Marcel Duchamp came from a family of artists – himself and his two brothers, Raymond Duchamp-Villion and Jacques Villon. The exhibition, as always at the Palazzo Grassi, is better studied in the catalogue than in the palazzo (half a dozen of their catalogues and you barely need to buy a book on art ever again).

In his early years Duchamp gambled through work in many styles – impressionistic, Fauve and Cubist. The Cubist paintings are clearly important, possibly brilliant. Then there are the works with glass. For many years a freestanding example of these called *A Bride Stripped Bare by Her Bachelors* stood in the Tate Gallery. The label with its title was fixed to the wall nearby; unfortunately, next to the label was a painting of a naked lady with a couple of fully dressed men looking at her. Who this painting was by I cannot remember but its association with the Duchamp label became the source of much misunderstanding and frequent complaints from those who take the trouble to complain about what they regard as pornography. There can be no confusion at the Palazzo Grassi, however, for a similar glass piece is clearly labelled – and not in the slightest erotic.

When you look at Duchamp's work you get the feeling that he had thought of everything that was to happen for the rest of the century, tried it and then tired of it. In 1918 he painted one last major picture, *Tu um*, then gave up painting and took up chess. After this he only made objects. William Rubin writing in his great book, *Dada and Surrealism*, said of this last oil: 'the elements splay out over the surface yet appear to hang together like a Duchampesque mobile'. It was Duchamp who later named Calder's sculptures 'mobiles'. After this work Duchamp thought that painting had had it – perhaps he was right.

NEWS ON THE RIALTO

WHEN Solanio (*The Merchant of Venice*, Act III, Scene I) asked, 'What's news on the Rialto?', the answer was not much, for in Venice there is never much that is new – yet perversely everything is new. Venice is a town that thrives on gossip, on trivia; isolated by water, complete in itself, self-centred, self-interested, it has its own rhythms, its own scale of import. The Venetian language – still widely spoken and totally different from Italian – has no equivalent of the English word 'privacy'. The closest they can come to it is 'intimacy', a word with a very different meaning. In fact, in Venice every small intimacy is treated to a great deal of local publicity – a town where always someone watches from a window, always someone listens from a nearby table.

The pace of Venice is modulated. Only the tourists hurry between churches and galleries: the citizens saunter, they greet each other. There is a rhythm to life in Venice that modern convenience has destroyed almost everywhere else: the changing seasons, the colour of the salads, the different fruits, the herbs. One month *castraourie* (the smallest of artichokes), the month before the *sepie* (baby black squid), the next month *bruscandole* (wild asparagus) made into risotto.

As the liturgical year progresses, the ringing of the bells changes, the colours of the sacraments change. The festivals of the people are tied to the Church and the availability of produce. All of this paces the life of the Venetian: the predictability of meeting a friend, or for that matter an enemy, in the street – then always gossip.

We sat in the Alla Madonna, the four of us – Paolo Zancope a dealer in 16th-century Venetian glass now, sadly, dead, my wife and I; and a painter and sculptor, Ludovico de Luigi, who paints pictures of the end of Venice, a Venice overcome by industry, a Venice destroyed by tourism. A recent work, first shown in St Mark's Square, had a slightly controversial career. A Deputy came from Rome to unveil it; all Venice was impressed. Unfortunately, the Deputy was Cicciolina, a former stripper elevated to Parliament, a lady more used to unveiling herself than sculpture – and this is exactly what she did. Naked, she sprang astride his great bronze horse.

The sculptor was torn between fear and delight – she looked wonderful on his horse – but the authorities tend to take a stern view of nudity in the town's main square. The crowd rioted - half for Cicciolina, half against – the horse, the artist, the Deputy all nearly destroyed in the crush. Then, however, they were saved by as near as is possible to a miracle: Cicciolina was wearing some very large plastic pearls, the string broke, the pearls rolled all over the pavement, the crowd pursued the pearls and the police restored order.

Someone had to be arrested. The Deputy was immune from arrest, so the artist found himself in court. The judge, a very attractive young woman, told him that he should have imagined that this would happen. 'How could I imagine that a Deputy would take her clothing off?' The judge replied: 'You are an artist, a man of imagination.'

'True,' said Ludovico, 'I can image you with no clothes on – but I cannot imagine that you will take them off.'

'If that is so,' said the judge, 'I can imagine you spending a year in jail for contempt of court.' Ludovico received, to his horror, a three-year suspended sentence.

The restaurant was packed; in the autumn there are few tourists, and the locals seem to have time to eat lunch. We gossiped on about events, and people, and we watched especially what they ate. We spoke of the forthcoming Carnivale and Ludovico's plan to cast his horse in chocolate (it weighed 500 kilos and the children ate the whole of it in seven minutes). We spoke of Venice's only bank robbery – where both the robbers and the police got lost in the maze of streets, in the end finding each other. The waiters all called Ludovico 'Maestro' and asked after his work; the artist in Venice is accorded a position in society as nowhere else. We ate *frittele* – very like a small doughnut, deep-fried, filled with crystallized fruit and pine nuts and a small quantity of *grappa*. What's news on the Rialto? – nothing much. The boundaries all over Eastern Europe were changing as we ate, but for the Venetian, other people's boundaries always change every 50 years or so. On the Rialto they think in millennia. What's news on the Rialto? – time and weather have washed Carpaccio's frescoes off its famous bridge.

INFILL TRAITOR

WHEN Napoleon came to Venice he did not come as a tourist, the way his countrymen do today. (The French are obsessed with Venice; few of them seem to go anywhere else.) He came as a conqueror, and in the manner of conquerors, he started to remove objects he found attractive – he had them crated up and sent back to Paris. The four Greek horses were among the treasures he sent home; these horses had already done quite a bit of travelling. The Venetians got possession of them when they sacked Constantinople, and the Turks had taken them from the Greeks. Wellington defeated Napoleon at Waterloo and the horses were sent back to Venice by a misguided Wellington – they would have looked wonderful in Trafalgar Square. They stood for many years above the portico of St Mark's, then they were put away in a small attic of the cathedral and replaced by fibreglass replicas. Napoleon admired St Mark's Square as well, but it was too large and too solid to dispatch home. He stood in that great square and remarked: 'This is the grandest drawing room in Europe!' He so admired it that he decided to build his office across one end; the only problem was that on the site of his proposed office building stood a rather fine church by Sansovino, the Venetian architect, and beside it a chapel by the same hand. This problem, however, was not insurmountable. Napoleon just pulled them down and started building.

Not everyone knows of this act of vandalism, and St Mark's Square is often quoted by conservationists as a great example of how if buildings are preserved our hearts can be lifted and our lives enhanced. As a result, architectural history stands still – in fact Napoleon was not the only vandal to have a hand in producing this marvellous square. St Mark's Square has been changing for the last thousand years, but I doubt if it will ever change again. Have we lost our self-confidence? Do we feel unable to produce great buildings? Do we lack the courage to improve masterpieces? Well, the answer to these questions is really of little importance. The truth is that today we ask the opinion of too many people. Few were consulted when Sansovino was commissioned to build his church and its chapel – and I doubt very much if Napoleon canvassed the citizens of Venice when he pulled them both down. The building he replaced them with is, in any event, totally out of keeping with

the other buildings in the square and fits in wonderfully. It has a neoclassical façade with generals from the ancient world parading along its frieze. There is an empty space – for which a sculpture was commissioned. But the Battle of Waterloo intervened, and Canova's statue of Napoleon never reached its appointed place – in the centre of the frieze that runs the length of what was his office block and is now in Correr Museum.

An exhibition of Canova's work opened in the neoclassical

interior of that building, but the statue of Napoleon was not included. I am told that it is hidden in a Venetian attic. Several dozen of Canova's works were exhibited, however, and very fine they were too, from great monumental works to the pair of small baskets of fruit carved in marble. The Three Graces were there, not the Three Graces lately moved from Woburn Abbey, nor a version of that sculpture, but a copy. There were three copies made of it, each identical. His classical figures are wonderful and the setting for them was perfect. There was a bust of Napoleon among them, looking like a classical god – no wonder Canova was his favourite sculptor. But when you see the portrait of Domenico Cimarosa, it becomes clear that Canova was more than just a sculptor who could fill an orangerie or carve a frieze, he was more than just a fashionable artist of the 19th century. There is a model of his tomb: the real thing is in the Frari, and is at last being restored, for it has suffered for some time from marble sickness, a kind of 'flu that causes the stone to distintegrate over a long period of time. I am very taken by his plaster casts with the nails still in them, nails that the men who carved these figures in marble used as reference points, for Canova often did not carve his own work.

Sadly for Canova, down the street – or rather the Grand Canal – was another exhibition, 'Leonardo and Venice'. Sure enough, there were a number of Da Vinci's drawings, small but beautiful things, coloured with a wash of the same shade as the ink in the drawing. A glaze introduced on to these drawings gave them a remarkable luminosity. What advertised itself as a show of the drawings of Leonardo had five paintings by Giorgione, including the *Three Ages of Mankind*. There were several sculptures by the Lombardo family and paintings and sculptures by other Venetian artists. Needless to say, Leonardo was the star. It was a testimony to him that his small drawings stood up to and knocked for six the works that surrounded them. Leonardo could do more with a few lines on a piece of paper six inches by four than Canova could do with a ten-foot block of marble.

CELTIC CROSSOVER

THE Palazzo Grassi is a very large palazzo indeed. It is not one of the most distinguished buildings on Venice's Grand Canal, indeed it is a somewhat cumbersome building, but converted to hold exhibitions, it has greatly improved. Gae Aulenti, the architect responsible for Le Quai d'Orsay in Paris, also carried out this conversion, and I must say that she has done a remarkable job on both these unpromising buildings.

The exhibitions at the Palazzo Grassi are financed by the Fiat car company and they appear annually. At first they seem to be exhibitions of the blockbuster kind, but on close scrutiny – or perhaps not such close scrutiny – they are something else. Long on information and short on objects in the exhibition is the formula that they follow. There is always a catalogue several inches thick and very heavy; you need strong arms to carry it home in the handy see-through plastic bag provided.

The exhibitions are always political. They promote one ideology or another: *Italian Art* or *The Origins of Venice* (the Phoenicians) are two of the recent ones. The exhibition *I Celti* was about Europe, one Europe. We were all European first and we will all be European last. This exhibition sets out to prove that the Celts were the first Europeans, records the parameters of that culture as it stretched from Hungary to the northernmost point of Scotland, from the late-Bronze Age to the 3rd century AD – truly the first time that Europe had a common culture, hopefully it will be the last. However much one may admire Celtic art, it is the very variety of Europe that makes the place interesting. The Celtic culture extended over this remarkable area and period of time because of the migration of peoples carrying a distinctive culture with them as they followed the deposits of the constituent parts of bronze in Europe – bronze they needed to make the art and artefacts of their daily lives. The Palazzo Grassi comprehensively recorded in its catalogue the progress of that migration.

The exhibition was different. Finding the Lindisfarne Gospels illustrated in the catalogue I rushed to see them. They were not there at all, but still safely in the British Museum. The famous bronze jugs were similarly still at home. There were in the British Museum alone perhaps a dozen Celtic masterpieces not included in the Palazzo Grassi. The exhibition was only a starting point for a pilgrimage around Europe *en route* to the many museums that house this culture; a trailer to whet your appetite.

A very large room in this palace was entirely filled with sinister fibreglass trees; a small golden craft sailed among them. The trees were black as the boat was gold. Gold, tiny and very, very beautiful. This large room, devoted to this tiny object with its theatrical presentation, gave the feeling of some ancient and unrevealed religion. It has all the mystery and impact its designers intended. Unfortunately, in the small print there was a footnote. This gold boat was not *the* gold boat at all – *the* gold boat was still in its museum in Dublin. Amongst the other absent objects was the Aesica Brooch found in 1884 at Great Chesters in Northumberland and now in the Newcastle-upon-Tyne Museum. Sir Arthur Evans, the great archaeologist who had himself dug up a great many works from antiquity, said of this brooch: 'It is probably the most fantastically beautiful creation that has come down to us from antiquity.'

Also not in this exhibition were any of the group of carved stone heads from Yorkshire, some two feet high, some only a few inches. These heads are to be found not in museums but still in the countryside, built into stone walls or the piers of gateways, owned by farmers who, out of superstition, kept them on their land.

The Celts were remarkable people, and their culture must surely be amongst the world's greatest. The Celtic world spans many changes in Europe. It extends from pagan times to that of the early Christians, and some of its best examples date from the early Christian period and are found in Ireland and northern Scotland. They include bell shrines and book shrines with intricate line patterns that show a sophistication seldom achieved since. These people were migratory people and they carried their art and artefacts with them, so of necessity – as with other migratory cultures – their objects tended to be small. The strange thing about the Celtic culture is that unlike most works of art that are distorted and often destroyed by magnification, the proportion and workmanship of these often tiny objects is so perfect they are improved by increasing their size. The poster for this exhibition showed the face of a goat in bronze. In reality it is less than an inch and a half high; in the poster it became two feet high and still looked wonderful.

This exhibition may have lacked many of the great masterpieces, but as I wandered through this vast palazzo, I saw no object that was bad or crude or poorly made. These people, the Celts, were truly the first Europeans showing a common culture, but, unlike Europe's current small club, they stood for something grander.

THE VENERABLE BEAD

ON the face of it 'new beads for old' might seem a pretty good deal, but not if those beads happened to be Venetian. Old Venetian glass beads have now become rare and valuable; a fact which is surprising, for at the end of the 19th century one in ten Venetians was engaged in making them – 16,000 tons in 600 different shapes and colours were produced each year. The beads of Venice were sent literally all over the world – to China, to Indonesia, to the Naga tribes of India and the Indian tribes of North America. They were exchanged for the goods that these people acquired mining or hunting. However, by far the greatest quantity were sent to Africa.

This trade in beads had been carried on by the Venetians since the 15th century – their earliest beads were small cubes of transparent glass, pink-tinged or deep blue like uncut diamonds or sapphires. Then a century later the fashion changed and chevron beads were made. Oval-shaped, their layers of coloured glass were faceted at the ends to form the V-shape chevron patterns that give them their name. The blue chevrons with the red and white lines were sent to Africa where today they are still dug from the sand dunes, giving some East Africans the idea that these beautiful beads grow in their continent's soil. The chevrons are the most valuable of the beads and vary in size from that of a green pea to a large goose's egg, although only three of these large beads are known still to exist. Red chevrons were sent to North America – red with black and white striped ends – and are perhaps the rarest and most valuable of all.

Now many of these antique beads have started to return to Venice where they are sold by Michele Pociello at his shop in the Frezzeria, which is filled with beads of different colours and shapes. I asked Michele how he became a bead merchant – 'by accident' he replied. I wondered what sort of accident could make a man take up such an exotic occupation – for Michele sells beads from all lands and all ages, and it is not exaggeration to say that he has trunkfuls. They come strung together fresh from the necks of tribal people. Michele sorts and then sells them to make necklaces for European women.

All this started when he was running a silver shop: 'I was in my shop when an African came in, and asked if I would buy some old beads that he had brought with him from Kenya.' Michele resold them the same day. 'I searched Venice till I found him and he gave me his address.' Michele then went to Africa and bought more beads from the man. In fact, to begin with he swapped new Venetian beads made by Moretti for old African-Venetian ones. As the trade in beads grew Michele contacted other dealers, his expeditions to Africa increased and he then started to go to India too. When the Indians saw the sorts of beads that Michele bought, they set about making brand new ones which Michele bought and then sold to those who could not afford the old ones. They sit in his shop, cauldrons of them, like so many brightly-coloured and wonderfully-shaped sweets.

Three years ago I started buying strings of beads that came from Africa from Michele. Every night I would sit at home and cut the strings, sorting each shape of bead into a pile. Then I sorted the contents of that pile into colours, putting each colour into a small white box. Within days my house was filled with small white boxes, each with its own colour and shape of bead. I found the work obsessive – you can't imagine my delight when I came across a particular bead that I had not expected in a necklace. Three years I spent sorting and stringing beads – I told my friends that I did this in order to be better able to contain my fury at the Chancellor of the Exchequer's handling of the British economy. The threading of tiny beads on to a string takes considerable concentration, and all other thoughts go from your mind except, I suppose, the seductive beauty of all these many-coloured beads, and thoughts of the necklace in a multitude of colours and shapes that you can make with them.

VENETIAN TRAWL

IN Venice, the gardens arrive by boat: large barges loaded with trees. This is one of the world's strangest sights. Even a couple as experienced in mobile foliage as Mr and Mrs Macbeth would have been surprised at the sight of one of these barges moving down the Venetian canals through the early morning fog with, on its decks, several fully grown *Magnolia grandiflora*, fruit trees – apples, pears, plums and damsons – and a large group of camellias, heavy with bud, ready for the first sun of spring, ready to flower.

Then Venice is a strange place, and the Venetians are used to the unusual. The mosaics in St Mark's Cathedral, recently restored and lit so that they can now be seen, have, among all the saints and angels, a portrayal of a rhinoceros – in the year 1230, when this mosaic was carried out, a creature of great novelty, an animal seen only by travellers to distant lands. Perhaps the Venetians were not convinced by descriptions of this animal, for the mosaic is tucked away, high in the roof of one of the aisles, a place of little prominence for such a rare and exotic creature. In the unicorn, perversely, they had total belief. The horns of two of these mythical beasts were kept in the cathedral and a small quantity scraped daily from them and fed to the doge to give virility, health and longevity. It seems to have worked in the case of Doge Dandolo, who in 1203, aged 96, was the first Crusader over the walls of Constantinople. The practice was discontinued shortly after this apparent success, as the horns were in danger of being nearly all eaten away by enthusiastic successors. The horn was actually the horn of the Narwhale, not as hard to obtain as that of the unicorn, but it cannot have been an easy item to lay hands on in the 13th century.

A few hundred yards from the great cathedral and St Mark's Square, the life of 20th-century Venice changes dramatically. The mass of struggling tourists ends – no more parties of Germans, squads of Japanese. Castello is possibly the only area left today that is still truly Venetian. Past the Arsenale and its assorted Greek lions with Celtic graffiti, over an iron bridge, down the Calle di Fornaio – so narrow that you go in strictly single file – out into the Via Garibaldi. This is a wide street; once a canal filled in by the Austrians in their – thankfully abortive – attempt to bring order to Venice. A street of market stalls selling vegetables and fish – just a few stalls. A street with a shop that sells freshly made pasta, a shop that sells ironmongery, a shop that sells ribbons, one of the best streets in the world for one reason only: this street has exactly the right number of people in it for its size. This street only sells products that people need for their daily lives. This street has the right number of trattorias, the right number of cafés. Incidentally, one of them sells the best sandwiches in Venice – sandwiches fuller and fresher than anywhere else. The balance of this street is perfect, yet it leads nowhere. As a canal it usefully led from the lagoon on one side of Venice to the lagoon on the other. As a street it has no purpose, so this great thoroughfare, which borders Venice's Biennale Gardens, is used only for shopping and talking.

On Sundays in the spring the people of Castello go to a restaurant called 'Vignole', on an island a few minutes away in a small boat. You can only go in a small boat, usually rowed, or powered by an outboard motor, for the water on the approach to this island is too shallow for larger craft. This factor dictates the kind of people who frequent the island and its restaurant. They are the working people of Castello and other parts of Venice – no tourists no speedboats. The island is basically a scrapyard, with every sort of rotting hull imaginable beached on the mud flats around it. Through this marine graveyard, where the parts of boats no longer usable are left to die, is a landing stage of the most primitive kind and moored to it are a cluster of skiffs and *topi al terzo* (small Venetian sailboats).

The restaurant is in an orchard: unruly grass and a few old trees, areas of bare earth that have proved popular spots for families to sit on previous Sundays, and a large shed – a shed filled with grills and cookers. The food runs the full gamut of the Venetian cuisine: from *risotto* to *fritta da mare*; heaps of cooked meats, heaps of cooked flesh without the benefit of a name; birds that would seem more appropriate to a London park than the dining table. But then at this restaurant the dining tables are a little primitive. Families sit on the ground or, if they arrive in time, on part of a remarkable collection of chairs at rough plank tables. They bring their own wine and some of their own food, buying what they need from the kitchen in the shed. Four or five hundred people come here on a Sunday. Mountains of food and, I dare say, a good few bottles of wine are consumed.

Families talk and argue. Lovers meet and, I suppose, on

occasions part here too. My host pointed out one fine-looking fellow. They call him 'Strangola'. He is, by trade, a strangler, but has a reputation for strangling people gently; girls of great beauty, grandmothers of vast proportions, young men and old!

It is one of the ugliest places that I have ever been to, but with time and wine and conversation, the blossom on the trees and the rotting hulks, it seems just as beautiful as the grandest efforts of Sansovino and Palladio.

ARRIGO CIPRIANI'S VENETIAN MAGIC

VENICE was made by collectors for collectors. They collected the objects and paintings; we collect memories of our visits there. Among their many qualities, the Venetians understood democracy. They controlled it and used it for future generations as well as their own – an uncommon attribute, illustrated by a sparkling jewel in the Venetian collection. I refer to Harry's Bar.

Harry's Bar is run by Arrigo Cipriani. For visiting American sailors, it is a bar; for the Venetian chic, it is a restaurant. It is amazing that this restaurant should attract so many local inhabitants. There are cheaper bars and grander restaurants. The food is not totally Italian, nor exclusively Venetian. The cuisine is Arrigo Cipriani's. Arrigo's father started Harry's Bar. The tale is well known from Ernest Hemingway's stories. He drank there between hunting trips in the lagoon to shoot the wild duck that land at night to rest while making their way to the warmth of Egypt. Hemingway ate the Carpaccio – a dish or paper-thin raw beef with mustard, named for the 15th-century Venetian master who have left the lagoon but whose paintings have travelled the world. Since the Hemingway days, Harry's Bar is a recipe that has been repeated often but equalled nowhere.

Collectors go to Venice to observe grand art and the art of the country, narrative art, and the art of Venice itself in the Correr Museum. But it is a city of frustration because nothing is for sale. I resolved this difficulty one day after lunch in Harry's Bar (risotto of vegetables, fish ravioli and meringue cakes) by beginning a collection of Harry's Bars.

So much had his father's name and reputation been used, that Arrigo once told me that he intended to take an advertisement in *The New York Times* stating that the only Harry's Bar he owned was the one in Venice. Since then, however, he opened Harry Cipriani's on the ground floor of the Sherry Netherland, a bar with a glimpse of Central Park. I was going to say it flourishes; this is the wrong word, for it is packed, with 400 customers on some days. But try as they will with Italian food and Italian chefs, the food is not the same. Arrigo commutes to New York but his heart and soul are Venetian. I go to Harry Cipriani's to escape America and dream of Venice. While I have eaten well in New York, the feeling that you are a favoured guest does not cross the Atlantic.

Moreover, the customers are ugly and not even Arrigo's great talent can arrange for them to be otherwise. Worse, their prejudices sit on the table, in the form of a small message stating that cigar smoking is discouraged. In Venice I puff smoke over his customers and they applaud me; they are a clique of connoisseurs who know a good thing when they smoke it.

In Venice, Arrigo can allow his great Italian ego to expand. In New York he has to adapt it to a curious morality that would ban smoking and insists that people eat small salads instead of heaps of pasta. These people drive away in limousines that blow filth into the atmosphere and do more harm in moments than my cigars can do in years. So this Harry's Bar is flawed and has no place in a fine collection.

Arrigo opened a second restaurant in Venice known as Harry's Dolci, as austere as the original, but with a view, for it looks out on the centre of Venice from the Giudecca. Although I am told that Venetians go there, no Venetian I know goes often. The food is good, the prices are good, the view is good; but it is a place for tourists, not collectors.

Only in Harry's Bar can a collector observe the subtle transformation from bar to restaurant; notice how no customer of standing is left without a table, and see how tables appear and are altered. This is the theatre of Harry's Bar. Across the lagoon is a hotel started by Arrigo's father. The Cipriani is a hotel of magnificence in a magnificent setting. But there is no magic in it now. Watch the magician himself, if it's magic you collect. See how Arrigo measures his clientele with a wave of the hand. Those he likes become disciples. Those he dismisses struggle to eat at his bar. (The best food, incidentally, is served while Arrigo is watching, possibly justifying the agricultural adage that the best manure is the farmer's boot.)

Arrigo's sister sits in Torcello, an island in the lagoon that houses some of the greatest mosaics in the world and a stone seat in which Attila once sat. The Locanda Cipriani is a *taverna* in the country side; tiny artichokes grow there, and it is for Sunday lunch or for dinner late in July when the nightingales are singing. But it is not part of a collection.

In Florence there is a Harry's Bar that belonged to some other Harry. I looked in once for a vodka on the rocks and found the atmosphere as cold as the River Arno in spring. There must have been several Harry's bars in the former Yugoslavia. The name appears in places like Sydney, Melbourne and Kuala Lumpur. In London there are two Harry's Bars, and it is wise to check which you have been invited to. One in Piccadilly copied only the name.

The second, in South Audley Street, belongs to Mark Birley, and it owes little to Arrigo, or any other Italian, except, perhaps, the chef. Michael, the manager, is Italian by extraction, but English by contamination, and he manages the restaurant with a style that is pure Mark Birley.

The collector sifts through the copies and the fakes, and imagined works by the master's hand, travelling the globe to obtain a full set, and returning always to the Calle Vallaresso by the San Marco *vaporetto* stop to eat pasta and drink *grappa* and understand that Harry's Bar without Arrigo Cipriani is like an orchestra without a conductor.

SEASONAL MEETINGS

THE whole summer Venice waited for the tourists to come, and then, with the first sign of autumn they were there – well, they weren't really tourists, they had travelled to Venice to attend four great events: the Architectural Biennale, the film festival, the annual meeting of Save Venice, and the Volpi Ball. How could a ball possibly be a great event? Well this one, quite apart from being held in Count Volpi's palazzo on the Grand Canal – a palazzo whose frontage covers an entire block – had about 1,100 guests. Very few people these days are able to give a party quite like the Count Volpi.

The Save Venice meeting had about 400 Americans attending it – as far as I could see they spent most of their time in the city wearing cocktail frocks and extremely high heels (the women that is). They travelled around the canals in a vast motor launch whose wash must have done the place a deal of harm. The film festival crowd kept very much to itself, isolated on the lido, most of their time locked in cinemas and the rest of it coming to terms with daylight. The women, in Ray Ban dark glasses and Louis Vuitton bags, had blonde hair and painted nails. The men – mostly balding – looked similar, but did not paint their nails. There was a touch of leather about both sexes. The architects at their biennale seemed to be everywhere and were immediately recognizable. There were thousands of them judging by those two weeks in September.

The extraordinary thing about this biennale was the uniformity of dress worn by those who attended it. The men were dressed from head to foot by Giorgio Armani, their sage green jackets had a casual but expensive look to them. White shirts buttoned right up to their Adam's apples, no ties, and on their chins a dusting of designer stubble. They all wore glasses – round with transparent frames – and I had the feeling that these did nothing to assist their eyesight one way or the other – and carried a plastic tube for drawings in much the same way as a senior military man carries a baton. The female of the species sported monks' habits in browns and blacks, or sometimes khaki; their hair was club cut, and what makeup they wore seemed to have been there some time. Their look was ecclesiastical – all wore black sandals with open toes.

For the first time in ages a new building has been built in Venice by a foreign architect, and what is more a British one – the late Jim Stirling's bookshop in the gardens was the centrepiece of the biennale. It seemed like some *bateau-mouche* removed from its journey up and down the stretch of the river Seine that passes through Paris, and left in the middle of a Venetian park. So here is the glass boat, complete with floodlights that illuminate the night sky – or at least for the first couple of nights. The authorities have switched them off now. Jim Stirling himself called it the boat shop – he claimed that it was inspired by the *vaporetti* that move the population of Venice from one place to another, but *vaporetti* have far less glass than this bookshop. This bookshop is definitely a *bateau-mouche* – as a bookshop, for me, it does not work: standing turning the pages of a book in a glass cylinder, however beautiful it may be, is not my idea of fun – I need ladders and shelves, benches and dust in any bookshop I am prepared to patronize.

The Swiss had an interesting pavilion. The work there by Herzog and De Meuron showed a great leap forward from the cuckoo clock. There was no sign of a Swiss Army penknife, the other great achievement of Swiss design, but instead rather large photographs of their work. It seems to me that exhibitions of architectural drawing are very limited in their use – architects make them to explain to builders how to build their buildings. These drawings have to read in the way a book is read – unlike paintings they are supposed to mean something, to convey a complicated message to people trained to understand that message. One of the reasons we have so many awful buildings is because the people who hire architects can very seldom understand their drawings and do not truly know what they are getting.

Instead of exhibiting architects' drawings you might just as well take a page of an ancient Chinese manuscript, enlarge it till the manuscript is several feet square, frame it and hang it on the wall – it would be as beautiful as many of the drawings in this biennale and just as incomprehensible. This exhibition is really only for the professional – or the totally ignorant who just like to look at shapes.

The Greeks also tried hard this year. Normally they arrive in Venice with a bundle of designs for rehousing the Elgin Marbles. This year, they decided to give this improbable dream a miss. The Greeks had a competition for the rebuilding of their pavilion in the Biennale Gardens. The designs were on the whole exciting, and a definite improvement on the existing pavilion – one scheme by a Christos Papoulias and Ioanna Theocharopoulou was very good.

The problem however is that the existing Greek pavilion is a listed building and cannot be touched in any respect.

The biennale is over now; all the pavilions stand closed in their gardens rather desolate with the leaves from the trees heaped in their doorways – and so they will remain until the next biennale comes around, or somebody thinks of another use in the meantime for this strange collection of buildings.

MURANO'S MELTING MOMENTS

MEN in overcoats, with scarves round their necks and trilby hats pulled down over their eyes – not in disguise, but rather as protection against the chill winds that come to Venice during the last days of winter; a visitor crossing St Mark's Square will certainly be approached by one if not several of these men. They sidle up to you in the most furtive of manners. 'Murano' they whisper. 'Murano?' the startled visitor replies. 'Murano glass – you wish to visit Murano and see our glassworks?' 'No, no,' the visitor protests; after all, the winter visitor to Venice has come to see the work of Palladio and Sansovino and the paintings by Titian, Tintoretto and Veronese. It is culture not glass that has drawn this visitor. Watching the lace-making and glass-blowing is for tourists. 'No, definitely NO.' The man in the camel coat and muffler, seeing no easier customers on the face of the rainswept square persists, and finally a compromise is arrived at. The visitor agrees to make the trip to Murano, and accepts from the glass-maker's persistent agent a free ticket on a motor boat to his factory. The agent begins to search for new customers and the visitor enters Florian's Café for a hot chocolate and a wastepaper basket to throw the ticket in.

Most serious people who visit Venice never get to see her glass – how wrong they are, for the soul of Venice is found amongst this glass, the truly horrible and the sublime sitting side by side on the shelf. Taken by the company's boat to Cenedese's factory – the glass companies like to take potential customers to Murano in their own boats for fear that the visitors might end up at the factory of their competitors. Just a smile at one of these men in overcoats puts you in the category of a customer. First you are shown a maestro at work. It all seems so terribly simple: a puff here and you have a glass balloon, flick of the wrist, and it becomes a plate. As the maestro works with the hot glass, it seems to have no colour other than that of the heat. As the glass cools the colours come, each one in the right place. The Japanese tourists flash their cameras, the bulbs exploding in unison. (The Japanese seem to have only the haziest idea of the state of Europe's climate, travelling at all the wrong times of year, spoiling completely the silence and desolation that Venice's winter visitor seeks.)

The temptation to miss the Japanese and therefore the maestro, going instead straight to the showrooms, is strong. Resist temptation, and watch the maestro at work long after the Japanese have left to make their purchases. Stay and watch the ballet of the glass-makers, as the rods with molten glass dripping from their ends pass from hand to hand. Each furnace is worked by two maestros who are assisted by eight apprentices; they weave between each other as they serve their masters, who sit on wooden thrones and roll the rods on the iron arms of these great chairs, shaping the glass with tongs. The timing has to be perfect and there must be no collision on the way to and from the furnace – the glass is only malleable for seconds. The Japanese tourists have be taken to the upper showrooms – Oh, horror! First thoughts are always correct. Here is room after room, shelf after shelf of coloured glass, each example more vulgar than the one before. 'Will you take a coffee,' Antonio Camarttie, Cenodese's master salesman, is at work. 'This is a decanter designed by Paolo Veronese – well, we don't know whether it was designed by him, but he used it in his painting *Supper in the House of Levi*. 'Will you take a little wine?' – he pours from a green bottle with a spring-held cap. 'This glass is also by Veronese'; he passes the wine. 'This,' he says, 'Tintoretto used this bowl in his paintings.' Titian, Giorgione, Bellini, Carpaccio, all the names of Venice are there on the shelves: glasses from the 14th, 15th and 16th centuries, glasses economic in their design, glass extravagant with twists and curls, colours subdued and colours vulgar, they are all there. Did they really use glasses like these in the Renaissance? Of course, in Venice everything was possible. The population became so extravagant in their tastes that sumptuary laws were passed to save them all from bankruptcy. Maybe it was the tales that Antonio told, but slowly the glass took on a sort of beauty as you moved from century to century; each design seemed to have its relevance.

'It's not all good,' says Antonio. 'Look at this horrible commissioned work, this is how they like it.'

I must confess, I liked it too – I held it in my hand. 'How much is this?'

'Two thousand pounds.'

'I had better put it down in case I break it.'

'Why, we will make another. Glass breaks, thank goodness – how else would we earn a living.'

SERMON IN STONE

THE deck of the vaporetto was a chilly place to stand. My fellow travellers – all Venetians – were well wrapped against the cold. The occasional gondola wandered on the Lagoon near the mouth of the Grand Canal. A large speedboat with giant engines – a stray from the French Riviera – lingered off the Piazzetta. Built of shining mahogany, with a ladder for swimmers to climb up over its stern to lie in the sun on the white vinyl cushions on its decks – this boat looked ridiculous in the winter weather. Its engines spat out smoke and canal water, all its power useless with nowhere to race. The vaporetto pulled away from this alien craft and headed for the Island of San Giorgio.

Once, when Venice was young, this island was called the 'Isola dei Cipressi'; it had vineyards, vegetable gardens, artisans' dwellings and a small church. Then in 1559 all that changed: Palladio started work on what many believe to be his masterpiece – the church of San Giorgio. On its façade a pediment surmounts

four columns whose bases stand many times the height of a man; its doorway is flanked by St George, a warrior, and St Stephen, a cleric. Palladio died in 1580, long before his work was finished, so he never saw the beauty of San Giorgio's tower and its pair of spires or its domes.

This day, the light in the church was cold except around the Great Altar which glowed with warmth; four priests and an Abbot stood before the altar, their purple Advent vestments reflected in the golden orb that bronze angels hold high above, the angels never so black, cold with winter light. To the side of the priests stood monks; the voices of the small choir hidden from view came and went as the responses passed from one side of the church to the other. The voice rose and fell, making their own music. Sometimes there was the feeling that they would fail, and the congregation stiffened with expectation, but they sang on, frail, soft, filled with calm, confidently aware of their own beauty. The service is extraordinarily austere, matching the church's hard, classical design.

The Abbot faced the altar and God, his flock behind him. He gave a spirited sermon. I do not understand a world of Italian but I loved hearing him speak, for like a bricklayer who mixes the cement that will hold his bricks together, he separated his words as with a trowel, then mixed them again, smoothed them off, divided them up, and mixed them yet again.

What a church this is: on each side of its altar is a great masterpiece by Tintoretto; Tintoretto's last work is in the chapel behind the altar called the Death Chapel; past the heavily carved choir-stalls up a winding stair is another chapel, and over its altar Carpaccio's *St George Slaying his Dragon*. However, this chapel is not famous for that wonderful painting, but rather as the only room outside the Vatican where a conclave has been held. On the death of Pope Pius VI in 1799 (he had been Napoleon's prisoner in Venice for many years and that emperor took a lively interest in who was going to be elected as his successor) the Cardinals met in that upstairs room as Napoleon sat in the apartments he had constructed across the end of St Mark's Square, a square he called the grandest drawing room in Europe. It took them from December 1799 until March 1800 to decide on Pius's successor.

This church and its monastery have seen much history. One of its Abbots was Henry Stuart, Cardinal Duke of York, the last of the Stuart line, and his name is written on parchment framed and hung on the wall of the room where the Cardinals met, along with the names of all the monastery's Abbots. Now his body lies at St Peter's in Rome with others of his royal race. Unsuccessful in their attempts to reclaim their thrones, they lie in a foreign tomb paid for by George III, the heir of their usurper.

As the congregation took the sacrament, the organ on its balcony high above the altar was playing for the first time during the service, the organist choosing strong, swift music by Vivaldi and his contemporaries. The congregation slowly returned to their seats and the Abbots sat for a moment in silent prayer; then he rose and blessed them, finally saying '*la messa è finita*'. At his words the organ broke into wild Baroque music and the priests, led by the Abbot, swept from the church like warriors, their purple robes flowing behind them. The organist played on, I could hear his music long after I left. Stepping down San Giorgio's steps to the piazza in front I halted. I could see all Venice before me, cold and proud, more beautiful than ever before.

Sabbioneta: Curtain-raiser

On the road between Mantua and Parma there is a stone gateway. This is no ordinary gateway but the Porta Imperiale, and behind it and its walls is a town to remember. The day I came to Sabbioneta the rain fell from the sky; I so nearly passed that most beautiful of places without another thought, ignorant of its existence. Curiosity, however, got the better of me – an open door of any sort is a temptation I cannot pass.

On the site of earlier fortifications, Sabbioneta was the inspiration of Vespasian Gonzaga, the head of a junior branch of the Gonzagas. He built a fortress greatly in advance of its age, and inside it a tiny, but carefully considered and complete, city. Why he built it in this particular part of Italy is something of a mystery.

Vespasian Gonzaga was a military man fascinated by artillery; perhaps he just indulged his interest in fortifications and talent for town planning or, like so many who are responsible for so much of the world's great architecture, just enjoyed building. Vespasian died in 1591, and the estate passed to his daughter who lived with her husband elsewhere. Sabbioneta fell asleep. The soldiers left and then the people – there was no reason for them to remain. Sabbioneta's walls crumbled, trees grew, and everywhere briars flourished.

In the mid-18th century the Hapsburgs occupied the town, then the French, then Hapsburg troops again. In the 19th century wandering scholars visited, and soon his secret and forgotten town became known as 'the little Athens'. Its buildings, much damaged by the soldiers of successive occupation, were by now used as store houses for grain and farm equipment.

In the 1960s the Italian government started restoration, and slowly a masterpiece has been uncovered. Sabbioneta is the most wonderful example of a provincial city. Where in Florence, Rome or Venice architects would have worked with grand materials, here they used paint, the most skilful of trompe-l'oeil. This town is a great city in miniature, with a castle, churches, Winter and Summer Palaces, squares, statuary, parks, houses for nobles and dwellings for those who served them, shops, hostelries and, most wonderful of all, a theatre.

When Shakespeare produced his plays at the Globe Theatre, his actors competed for attention with rowdy crowds on an open stage.

The citizens of Sabbioneta sat in their court theatre surrounded by frescoes in the style of Paolo Veronese. The actors played beneath a proscenium arch. Behind the audience is a great colonnade topped with statues in the antique style; between its arches paintings of more statues, each standing in its own portal. Along the walls, noblemen and their ladies look down from balustraded balconies in the style of Veronese's work at the Villa Maser. Supporting these balconies are classical arches through which the landscapes of northern Italy can be seen, and nestling in these landscapes, spires, columns, domes, ruins, and the fortifications of hill towns – all the work of a painter.

The grandest church stands in the Piazza Ducale, its façade dramatically styled in zigzag patterns of white and pink Verona marble. The Ducal Palace is across the square. Luckily, damage to it seems to have taken place only as high as a man can reach. There is room after room of the most exotic painted ceilings. Behind the palace is the church of the incarnation of the Blessed Virgin, an octagonal building. As you look up you see a great dome, the trick of a craftsman's brush. Over the altar is the statue of Vespasian by Leone Leoni, a work of great quality, comparing this Gonzaga Duke with the Roman emperor whose name he took. Leoni was a pupil of Michelangelo and his portrait owes much to his master.

A short walk away is a splendid building perhaps 300 feet long, a colonnade underneath, a gallery above, its walls painted with busts of Roman generals and trophies of arms. Nearby is the Summer Palace, an enchanted place, room after room filled with the vitality of its paintwork. As I stood in a painted room I looked out at a garden of crumbling walls and earth heaped untidily; weeds growing everywhere. I knew why I loved this place, for the strongest human instinct is to improve – if this place could be improved, restored, put back to just how it had been 400 years ago. For myself, I hope it stays much as it is, for the joy here is of what might have been, and to dream of what it all might be again.

FOUR

WEST TO EAST

WHAT REIGNS IN SPAIN

BARCELONA is a good-looking city. Modelled on Paris, it is a city where time has stood still. At the beginning of this century it was largely rebuilt in the style fashionable at the time, each wealthy family competing to build grander and flashier monuments to their success. The perfect patrons of architecture. General Franco, finding that Catalonia was the last bastion of Communist resistance in Spain, never forgave the region. As a result, no government investment was made in the area. Barcelona has few new buildings and consequently few old buildings have been pulled down. The city therefore has the most remarkable collection of late-Victorian architecture.

Travellers leaving Barcelona airport by taxi on the way to the city centre will pass wide avenues lined with trees, and circumvent great roundabouts with sculptures or fountains at their hearts. Should they ask their taxi driver 'what is worth seeing in Barcelona?' he will not reply 'you must look at Gaudí's buildings' or 'do not miss Las Torres de Avila…' The latter, incidentally, is no medieval castle, but a nightclub designed by two architects called Arrivas and Mariscal, set in the walls of a plaster castle which is itself part of the completely horrible imitation town built for the 1929 World Fair, and without charm of any sort. This nightclub, however, is remarkable; an example of contemporary design that demonstrates all the fantasy of Gaudí and Miró, a building fully in the tradition of this adventurous town. A town that at the same time as it was constructing this horrible miniature Disneyland, was building Mies van der Rohe's Barcelona Pavilion. Pulled down after the end of the World Fair, it was rebuilt just a few years ago from plans and a few photographs, which, of course, were taken in black and white. No one knows how accurately the original colours of the three marbles used have been reproduced, or if the red velvet curtain was quite that red. Nevertheless the result is remarkably beautiful. A pavilion, or a sculpture that you can walk and sit in? Hard to tell. I doubt if it matters, as a building it enhances the life of all who see it.

How remarkable that Barcelona should have been rebuilding the work of one the world's greatest architects at about the same time that public opinion was being mobilized – with great success – to stop the building of what was perhaps his masterpiece in the City of London. Barcelona, however, shows no fear of the new. Barcelona – careful of its past – is hellbent on reaching the future.

Several great artists have museums exclusively to themselves: The Fundació Miró, by the same architect as the Foundation Maeght in the South of France, is an exciting building with good pictures. The Palacio Berenguer d'Aguilar, the Picasso museum, is a boring building with sensational paintings. Between 1954 and 1960 Picasso engaged himself on a series of paintings, reworking subjects by Great Masters. Here are several dozen works from the 'Las Meninas' series (the original by Velasquez). They are stunning.

It must be a sculpture by Picasso.

Barcelona, however, is foremost a city of architecture, and the best known of her architects is Antonio Gaudí. Descended from generations of potters, Gaudí used ceramics in his work with an enthusiasm and a facility that could only come from such a background. His buildings are fantastic in concept and remarkable in detail: broken tiles reassembled; swirls of coloured mosaics; carefully carved wooden doors with exactly cast bronze fittings. La Pedrera – a block of flats inspired by the strange rocks about an hour's drive from Barcelona – is a building that the Flintstones would feel at home in. In one block in the Passeig de Gràcia, there are three different houses: the Batilló House by Gaudí, the other two – Casa Lleó and Casa Amatller – by different architects, and each as remarkable as the other.

Gaudí's name is synonymous with Barcelona. Even as an old man 74 years old, he was still working. When he was knocked down by a tramcar he was taken to be a pauper because of his clothes and, unrecognized, he was carried to the Hospital Sant Pau, a hospital built by his rival Dominechi Montaner. After three days he died, his greatest work – the Church of the Sagrada Familiar – still unfinished. Exotic and frightening, the parts of this building by Gaudí's own hand are filled with majesty. Its great towers and the freshness of the Rosary doorway demonstrate a range of talent seldom seen in architecture of any other period. The parts built from his plans after he died are ponderous and uncertain. The building – still less than one quarter built – continues. Perhaps with time those responsible will be able to catch the spirit of Antonio Gaudí.

Then time is the enemy of many great churches. The cathedral in Barcelona, in its third incarnation, was started in 1298; work was interrupted in 1422, and it was finally finished in 1887 when the main façade was built according to the plans that the French architect Mestre Carlí had drawn up when he was commissioned by the city council in 1408.

'What is there to see?' our traveller asks the driver of his taxi. Without hesitation he replies, 'you must see Snowflake'.

'Snowflake?' the traveller queries.

'Snowflake,' the driver repeats, 'at the zoo. He is the only albino gorilla in the world'.

HAMBURGER RELISH

A GRAVE error would be made were I to suggest that Hamburg is a modern city; a new city, yes, for most of it was demolished by Allied bombing, but modern no – not in its layout nor in its style, for Hamburg has been rebuilt much in the way it was before the war. Never a truly beautiful city as Rome, London or Paris are, Hamburg is a provincial city and that is how it looks and how it is – built around two lakes, one large, the Aussenalster, and one small, the Binnenalster. Hamburg has some sort of beauty – the beauty that you might find in Geneva or Stockholm, but bear in mind that Stockholm has some distinguished buildings, and as far as I could see Hamburg has none.

I was young when I first visited Hamburg, and with the enthusiasm of youth I headed – as soon as I could respectably finish my work – to the St Pauli district. The joys – I found them so then – and the delights were in the Reeperbahn – a street near the port named after the ropemakers who once worked there. Perhaps it should have taken its name from the sailors and ladies who entertained them there – for they have abounded in that district for the last 150 years, while you cannot find a ropemaker to save your life.

On a recent visit I found that street and the alleys that surround it are just as seedy as they always were. The difference for me is that this time I realized how awfully shoddy and second-rate this district of cheap delight is. There is one difference in St Pauli from the days of my youth – a museum has opened at 69 Bernard-Nocht-strasse – just around the corner from that other long-running exhibition in the Herbertstrasse, a street where ladies of a certain lack of virtue sit in shop windows without having bothered to dress completely. The new museum, predictably I suppose, is the Hamburg Erotic Art Museum. This is not at all a shoddy affair; housed in a converted warehouse, it contains much that can truly be called art – several very fine paintings by Allen Jones come to mind, a set of Japanese erotic prints are also well-worth looking at, but for the rest it is the sort of art where so much imagination has been used by the artists that there is no need for those who would view their work to use any at all.

The day was cold, the people seemed glum, the streets were decorated for Christmas – twinkling lights everywhere. The shopping district of Hamburg, these days a mass of interconnecting arcades, were busy, the shops filled with goods, but the population seemed to be looking not buying – the prices were high due in some part to the value of the mark but also to the general condition of the country. In any event, the citizens of Hamburg did not seem intent on beating the Christmas rush. Many shops were selling clothes – boutiques stocking the famous brands. I was intrigued by one that sold only model ships and planes – most of them a couple of inches long; they must surely have in stock a model of every craft in the world. Then there were those selling craft-like goods – stock that has that home-made look about it – manufactured in the factories of Mexico and the Philippines. These shops have about them a curious smell – a smell that is supposed to indicate that everything on the premises is made from environmentally-conscious materials. A smell that will bring good luck and good health to your home and hide the fumes of cooking – a smell composed of candle wax, fir cones and stale pot pourri – the most repellent smell in the world, and what is more you find these awful shops all over the world selling the same goods. I cannot resist going into them and the smell gives me hay fever.

On the streets, Hamburg has its share of beggars – Eastern European women sitting on the best sidewalks, their heads shrouded, bowed as if in shame or perhaps despair. Often they hold their babies, sitting hunched up as if trying to avoid notice yet desperate to attract the gift of a few coins. I dined at Peter Lempeke's restaurant where Germans dine. The restaurant was packed – and Mrs Lempeke made a table for me in her hall. I ate soured herrings and roast goose and I noticed parties of German men dining together. But there was no joy in there, no exuberance nurtured by food and drink and the warmth of Peter Lampeke's restaurant.

I had walked at lunchtime among the Christmas stalls set up around St Petri's church – stalls selling toys and Christmas goods – stalls selling drink and food. As I walked amongst the crowds gathered in this market I found them subdued – quiet and I supposed a little mystified. For these were the children who had set out after the war on a new path – the past, too horrible to remember, put from their minds by the work of building a future; their nation became wealthy and in time their nation was reunified.

This was what they had dreamed of, but where was paradise? In a few short months all had changed – gone was the land of milk and honey. Their economy in which they had taken such pride no longer prospered, the marriage with East Germany that they had longed for seemed in reality far less attractive than it once seemed and now a shadow of that forgotten past, a ghost they believed well laid, a spectre had appeared at the feast: racism and violence. The Nazis are not just history and the shadow of their violence, the burning of hostels, the harassing of foreigners and even murder, hangs over the normally exuberant city of Hamburg.

HOME IS WHERE THE ART IS

THERE are few, if any, palaces in the world as beautiful as
Schönbrunn on the outskirts of Vienna. When built, the palace and
its grounds were more extensive than the city itself and they are
still larger than the state of Monaco. A palace with 1441 rooms, of
which 139 were kitchens, it housed and fed a court of about a
thousand officials and functionaries.

On the face of it the palace seems gigantic, but that is not the
feeling you get as you walk around. Instead, it is not at all hard to
understand how Marie-Antoinette missed Schönbrunn when she
moved to Versailles. Try as she might, Versailles defied her
attempts (the building of the Petit Trinon and the Hameau) to
create a feeling of homeliness like that of Schönbrunn, which has
an intimacy that even 270 bombs, considerable rebuilding and all
the bureaucracy of the Austrian Civil Service has failed to destroy.

As you walk in the garden after the style of Le Nôtre or stand in
the bedroom of 19th-century Elizabeth of Austria you feel that this
was a family home. Despite the fact that Elizabeth owned 250 pairs
of gloves and thousands of dresses, kept in rooms hidden in the
core of the palace, and the Habsburgs were a pretty grand family –
indeed they still are – they were a family nevertheless.

The rooms are furnished austerely, but the bed that Emperor
Franz Joseph slept in is still there, as is the screen that kept the
draught from his shoulders as he sat at his desk – Franz Joseph was
so obsessed by fresh air that he kept his study windows wide open.
Portraits of Hapsburgs hang everywhere – the bombs did not do as
much damage as might be imagined, for the Austrians were
expecting them long before Allied bombers flew over Vienna, and
the Germans had packed up not only the pictures and furniture,
but wall paintings, panelling and even parquet flooring. The crates
containing Schönbrunn's fabric were dispatched to long defunct
mines until after the Second World War when, as if from a deep
sleep, the furnishings were returned to the reconstructed shell of
the palace, where they are today as if they had never been removed.

The Chinese room has painted panels of white figures on a blue
background – their limbs picked out in fluorescent paint. In the
dim light of candles the figures glow, and as the flames flicker they
seem to move. The room of 17th-century Indian miniatures is
perhaps the finest rococo room in the world. With its panelling

infilled by Indian miniatures it is a masterpiece and yet a tragedy; for the miniatures, cut to fit the room's ornate shapes, are among India's most important examples of the miniaturist's art, bought from the maharaja who collected them when he fell on hard times.

Off the ballroom are two black lacquer saloons; the one used by the Empress Maria Theresa has a secret stairway to her chancellor's apartment. She could entertain an important visitor in her salon and the court would never know that the chancellor had also been present. A table hidden in the parquet floor would rise at the touch of a button for maps to be laid out or for treaties to be signed. Then there is the room which gives no hint of its purpose except for plaster-cast musical instruments in each corner of the ceiling – horns, violas, trumpets. This must surely be the most famous of music rooms. Schubert and Schumann played here, so did Brahms, Liszt, Beethoven and Strauss. What musical history was made in this room where the six-year-old Mozart, enthused by the applause at his playing, ran and jumped on to the Empress Maria Theresa's knee. The court watched in horror to see how she would react to this uninhibited display.

Now the musicians are gone and the deathmask of Napoleon's only son, the Duke of Reichstadt, lies in a glass case. He lived and died here, and beside his childish face is a bird, now stuffed, that he is said to have played with in Schönbrunn's gardens. This palace was truly once a home, even if now it is a palace of ghosts.

There's no Place like Prague

PRAGUE is by repute a fairy-tale city, one of the most beautiful cities in the world – if not the most beautiful, or so men say. The city has been held in two time warps: first that of the Austro-Hungarian Empire, when Prague was subservient to Vienna, though they were similar cities in a way: Vienna land-locked but astride the Danube, Prague situated on the river Vltava. That is where the similarity ended. Vienna was the capital of a great empire, the home of an enormous bureaucracy which grew and became a centre of culture, a great metropolis that set fashions in art and music for the world to imitate; home to emperors and empresses, their armies, their courts and all who surrounded them. Prague was forbidden by decree to demolish its city walls. Unable to grow, it found little opportunity to rebuild.

During the second of these time warps, Communism, the city barely developed. The old town, the palaces and churches

More Baroque than role ZZ

survived. Some attempts were made to restore them – attempts that extended as far as keeping the weather out, but money was mercifully short and thank goodness it still is. 'One of the most beautiful cities in the world' – it's hard to substantiate this claim. Prague is a fairy-tale city in the sense that Disneyland is a fairy-tale. Like Disneyland, Prague has its crowds, and very impressive these crowds are – in fact they make the hordes that visit Venice seem a mere smattering of tourists. Just like Disneyland the city of Prague is a vast retail premises with shops that sell the goods tourists like to buy – the craft-like products that you find from John O'Groats to San Francisco. As for shops that sell clothes and other goods, they are few and far between.

In Prague it is in the streets that the selling is done – stall after stall in street after street – and these stalls you will find (that is if you can fight your way through the tourists to get close enough to look at them) sell only four different items. First there are Russian dolls, the swollen wooden dolls – sometimes as many as 14 – that live inside each other: dolls painted as peasants, dolls painted as politicians. Then, of course, there are Red Army wrist-watches, the watches of different ranks for different prices, and hats to go with them; fur hats with red enamel stars at their fronts or peaked caps with gold stars, their centres picked out in red enamel, or, a great rarity, a fighter pilot's helmet. I was also offered his flying suit with all the attendant piping and buckles. And then there are the inevitable tins of caviar. I do not want to sound blasé about a product as delicious as caviar, but the endless stalls with endless jars do leave you with the feeling that this product is not quite as exclusive as the head waiters in the world's better restaurants would have you believe. Caviar is very cheap these days in Prague. I ate a lot of it – some delicious, some so salted it was almost inedible. To buy caviar from these stalls is to play Russian roulette – with salmonella poisoning taking the place of the single bullet in the revolver. Caviar has to be carefully kept or it becomes lethal.

To walk at night across the Charles Bridge that spans the Vltava river between the new and the old town is truly wonderful – despite the crowds who come to see the floodlit castle, the towers of the churches and the spires of the new town. It is all a bit like a stage set, the buildings mostly Baroque, very like the gingerbread houses that you find in the windows of that famous Viennese coffee house,

Demel. There seems to be something false about the whole place –
a giant theatre built for the puppets that hang in many of Prague's
shop windows. These puppets really are strange; they come in all
sizes from an inch or two high to several feet – there are witches
and devils, skeletons and evil spirits, but none with the beautiful
smiles of the cherubs that gamble amongst the rococo swags and
swirls of the city's churches. No, the faces of these small stringed
figures come from a culture far older than that of Prague, a barbaric
Northern culture, a trace of which can be found in the National
Museum, housed in the Lobkovic Palace, part of Prague Castle.

There, amongst a thousand and a half minor treasures of the
Czech's nation's past, is a remarkable object, an object that is truly
a masterpiece – the head of a Celtic man from Msecke Zehrovice.
Carved from limestone in the second century AD, this head has a
broad nose, bulging eyes and curling moustache; around its neck is
a great torque, the symbol of a chieftain. It is one of the most
important Celtic sculptures in the world. In the face of this Celtic
man and the puppets there is a great strength and beauty not found
in Prague's baroque conceits.

PICKING UP THE PIECES

THE greatest jigsaw puzzle in the world lies at Akrotiri on the island of Santorini in the Cyclades. It consists of thousands of pieces of broken pottery. The man charged with putting together this vast puzzle is Professor Doumas – in one ancient cupboard alone his archaeologists found over 400 pots.

The first human settlement at Akrotiri was in 3200 BC but the period that chiefly concerns Professor Doumas is the 15th century before Christ, when a volcano erupted and encased the town in lava. Unlike Pompeii, the town had been warned of its end by a series of earthquakes. The population fled, taking their treasure with them and leaving only pottery (most of it, from the point of view of fine art, quite boring) and the frescoes on their walls – in contrast works of amazing quality. Helped by these fragments the team has traced the history of this distant people: what they ate, how they lived, the nature of their trade. Each piece of the puzzle will slowly be put together over the next hundred years. I saw a sheet of dusty plastic pulled back to reveal a fresco of incredible beauty, 3000 years old, reassembled from the scrapings of paint.

The Cycladic islands, for the most part bare of all except the rudiments of agriculture, now have a booming tourist industry. One reason why people come here could be a desire to observe the activities of the likes of Professor Doumas. True, they visit the archaeological sites in large numbers, but these islands hold something far more precious for the tourist – the chance to travel and yet feel securely at home. A familiar accent in every square for the British tourist; a national tongue for the Germans, French and Italians; restaurants that call themselves pubs and sell meals for the unadventurous palate and shops that make no demand on either the tourist's taste or his wallet, selling goods that always look worth more than they cost. There are always the same shops on every island, the same goods for sale; goods that it is hard to imagine anyone wanting to buy or possibly needing. Cheap luxury this – the very stuff of tourism. And most important of all for the tourist: more tourists – to jostle against, to drink with and offering the chance to make friendships that last a holiday. The stark beauty of the islands – with their white buildings picked out in blue, small churches and windmills – are just a stage set for this activity.

There seems to be a distance between the tourists and their

surroundings, each hardly aware of the other. Only one island escaped tourism and that is the pilgrim site of Tinos, one of the most holy in the Orthodox Church. Tourists and pilgrims tend not to mix: tourists put up the prices and pilgrims spoil the fun.

Across these much-fought-after ancient islands lies the skeleton of the Venetian conquest. For over 400 years, Venice ruled here; leaving her lions over gateways, portraits of her Doges and, in the square of Heraklion, a fountain of incomparable beauty. A Venetian may feel like the Japanese official who visited England at the beginning of the century and was taken to a stately home and shown their Japanese Garden. What did he think of it? 'We have nothing like this in Japan,' he replied – and so it is with the fountain in this square. A brass band plays tunes from *The Music Man* in the early evening and tourists and locals sit drinking coffee. The cafés advertise hamburgers, spaghetti and sauerkraut. Everywhere you find traces of Venice, though none of them as beautiful as the traces of ancient Greece in Venice.

In Delos, as in all the ruins elsewhere on these islands, it is not so much the beauty of the individual works of art that strikes you, because most have been destroyed or taken to museums; nor is it what was once there, for reconstructions, models and architectural perspectives of what once existed are rather dull. It is the presence of these places that has the impact: an invisible form of beauty hidden distant in the memory of man, it is its stirring that excites us. Ravaged by nature, torn apart by unappealing tourism, where myth begins and reality ends: such is the magic of these islands.

I Looked Over Jordan

SCHOOLBOYS of my generation were brought up on images of Arabia, of Lawrence, Glubb Pasha, desert soldiers with crossed bandoliers and flowing robes (for those of a higher turn of mind, the images came from the Bible). The land, crossed by Greeks and Romans, French and English, has left its imprint indelibly on our culture. Now Jordan has left its imprint on me as the most recent addition to my collection of places.

It is the home of Petra, 'rose-red city half as old as time', that remained undiscovered until the early 19th century when a Swiss explorer heard rumours of a hidden city and was allowed by the desert tribes through the narrow crevice that is the entrance to Petra. They let him stay only one day, but it was long enough for him to record the great tombs, the caves where people dwelt, the remains of the Roman forum, and the ruts cut by chariot wheels in the stone pavement (incidentally, the chariots drove on the left-hand side of the road).

This strange town was not built but carved from the rock by the Nabaetine people in the first 100 years after the death of Christ. Rich through trade they imported Greek and Roman architects to build their great monuments. Now the trade is in tourists. On my first night there I walked down the narrow defile that is still the entrance with thunder echoing round me, and saw the great building they call the Treasury lit for moments by flashes of lightning.

How strange this relic of the long-gone Nabaetines seemed, for it is a monument to a people whose very name means to look outward, to accept innovation and change. In Petra traders exchanged the spices of the Far East for the furs of the North. Now they sell coloured sand, cleverly arranged in patterns and bottled. In spring Petra is carpeted by wild red tulips and later in the year with great clumps of tall white alliums.

Jordan, where being stuck in traffic on the busy long, straight road to Aquaba means looking at scenery that has not changed for 2000 years. The ridges of the black bedouin tents are like ripples in the ocean, and the shepherds still herd their flocks of camels, goats and sheep. Nowhere is the contrast between ancient and modern better expressed than in the town that surprised me most, for Jerash is regarded as the most complete Roman city outside Italy.

Yet only one-third of it has been excavated; the rest is buried beneath a Palestinian refugee camp. Walking down a mile-long colonnade on a Friday I could hear the muezzin calling people to prayer across the valley. Each column of the colonnade was given to the city by a citizen whose name was inscribed upon it.

There is much to be learned in Jerash. In the Temple of Dionysus, for example, where, after it had become a Christian church, worshippers would bathe in great pools and once a year the priest would amaze the populace by re-creating the miracle of turning water into wine. Modern archaeologists have discovered a hidden pipe leading to the vats of wine, and the tap the priest turned to work his transformation. At the Temple of Artemis, where the tall columns are so finely balanced that they sway in the wind, larders have been found hidden deep in the earth where sacrificed animals were stored by gourmand priests for their own private consumption. And in the theatre, where the acoustics are so perfect that a whisper can be heard clearly in the back row, the stage could be flooded to become a swimming pool where perhaps a Roman Esther Williams swam at the direction of an early Busby Berkeley. One Roman was not impressed. When the Emperor Hadrian visited Jerash he looked around and suggested to the mayor that he ought to rebuild the town gates. Too small, said the Emperor.

Jerash became part of Byzantium and its temples became churches, but its remains still exert an influence. The architecture is bold and unembarrassed by scale. This is architecture built for a certain future, making no cringing curtsies to the past.

KEPT IN RESERVE

THE Middle East is not unfamiliar with warfare. For centuries past, man has fought over its fertile valleys and deserts, has built monuments and destroyed them. Towns and cities have been consumed by warfare and rebuilt in the image of the conqueror. Great cities have been destroyed by earthquakes, peoples destroyed by famine and pestilence. In the heart of this region lies Basra, the site of the Garden of Eden, the beginning, perhaps, of life on earth. What is certain, however, is that the valleys of the Euphrates and Tigris rivers meet here: valleys that have become the flyway for millions of migrating birds, birds that journey from Europe far into Africa, birds that travel each year from Russia to northern Australia, birds as diverse as the white stork and the small warbler. While man is ingenious enough to improve upon destroyed architecture, and his hands are supple enough to manufacture broken artefacts anew, he has no means of replacing a lost variety of bird.

This desert area of Iraq is of particular natural importance, the meeting point of the European and Arabian species. The brown bear, seldom found now in Europe, the Arabian wolf, and many other interesting and beautiful animals and birds. The irony of the destructive attack upon Kuwait by Saddam Hussein, the disastrous consequences of the action necessary to remove him, is that this area was one of the few places in the world making great efforts to repair some of the ravages of the 20th century by restoring locally extinct species to their original habitat. A small group of the extremely rare Sommering's gazelles, along with many other animals in the Old Botanical Gardens of Kuwait City, have been shot by soldiers from Iraq. However, it is the loss of the plans of the Kuwaiti Government to establish a National Park along the border with Iraq that is the real tragedy – a park where they intended to reintroduce the Houbara bustard and the Arabian gazelle, a desert reserve to which many of the species now extinct in this region would return. It must be hoped that, with the rebuilding of this region, these plans will not be overlooked and attention paid only to the provision of motorways, hospitals and schools.

In Saudi Arabia, the Government has set up a centre for the conservation and breeding of many of its endangered species, with the intention of returning them to the wild. There are, in the centre, well over a thousand of some of the world's rarest animals:

sand gazelles; Arabian gazelles; the Saudi Dorcas gazelle, extinct in its habitat; the Saudi wolf; and the Ruppell's fox, a small and rare sand fox. Then there is the Arabian oryx, the most beautiful mythical unicorn, for, when seen in profile, its long, sweeping horns seem as one. It was an animal hunted for 3000 years by desert warriors and it survived. But no antelope, however agile, was equipped to withstand the advent of the automatic rifle, and the early 1960s saw its demise outside captivity. This research centre in Riyadh, on the other hand, has prospered, and the number of these rare animals has increased. There are several zoos with important collections in Israel, and the Tel Aviv University Wildlife Research Centre has done much work for conservation, and cares for many rare animals. In Oman, meanwhile, repatriation of desert antelopes has started. There is now a wild population of the Arabian oryx, the descendants of captive-bred animals returned to their habitat. Another population of this elegant animal is in Jordan, and there are plans for a reserve on the Jordanian/Saudi border. All of this work goes on in the world's most volatile region.

These animals are in great danger. In the early 1960s, small groups of antelopes were caught and taken to zoos in America and Britain: the addax, short-legged, beige and corkscrew-horned, now thought to be extinct in the wild; the Dhana gazelle, long-legged and long-necked, of which less than a thousand remain; the scimitar-horned oryx, another antelope extinct in its natural habitat. The subsequent civil war in Chad and the famines that sprang from it, combined with high-powered military rifles, has proved the wisdom of this action. These zoos have become a Noah's Ark for these animals, places where they can be bred and studied. London Zoo is one of the organizations active in this field. It has an almost unique expertise combining fieldwork and research.

Zoos are no longer animal prisons. In their modern form, they can be havens of safety. The scarce resource of these rare and extremely beautiful animals, spread among them on a planned basis, means that neither disease nor war will ever destroy them completely. For man being the aggressive beast he is, it is unlikely that the war against Saddam, or for that matter any other war, will end all wars, and we had better take good care of our zoos so that our zoos at least can take care of the world's birds and animals, after terrible carnage, ready to play an important part in rehabilitating our planet.

FIVE

EXPRESSLY ORIENTAL

CHERRY-GO-ROUND

THERE are certain places and events that seem to have become the property of the tourist: Windsor Castle, Versailles, the Tower of London, the Changing of the Guard at Buckingham Palace, the Venice Carnivale – the list is endless. This is a shame, for each of these is remarkable in itself – well worth the struggle to see, well worth fighting your way past the massed ranks of tourists who stand in front of a picture at Windsor, or at Hampton Court listening to a strident guide. Well worth too the crowds at the Tower of London – which has the largest number of tourists visiting any site in the United Kingdom – for even a glimpse of the collection of arms and armour, a collection which is possibly among the best in the world.

There are other places – for example the Louvre, the British Museum and the Metropolitan Museum in New York – which although they have a large number of tourists do not spring to mind in this context. There are events like the Derby and the Palio at Siena where you would expect large numbers of tourists. The Derby is basically a day out for Londoners, and the Palio an event for the Sienese which they take with great seriousness. Heaven help the hapless tourist who should pass a casual remark about the lack of flesh on any of the horses. A tourist in the wrong place is likely to be trampled by one of the several flagwaving and drum-beating phalanxes of locals. These are strictly events for the inhabitants.

The cherry blossom season, which in good weather lasts three or four days at the best, would seem to be a tourist trap thought up by some more-enterprising-than-usual government body. An event for the purpose of persuading tourists to visit Japan. The cherry blossom is taken seriously by all from Emperor to doorkeeper. I do not know how the Emperor celebrates Hanami (the best day for blossom viewing), but doorkeepers all over Tokyo, and I suppose Japan, are sent out early to reserve a tree. They spread a tarpaulin on the ground and surround it with tapes stretched between piles of stones. About midday they are joined by groups of workers from their offices. These groups then spend the rest of the day drinking sake and eating, pausing only to sing and dance. The same practice is carried out in the evening despite the fact that it is dark and you cannot see the cherry blossom. The Japanese regard the cherry tree with a reverence similar perhaps to that with which the British once regarded the oak. There is no doubt that the blossoms of Japan are very beautiful; amongst the most beautiful being *Prunus* 'Shogetsu' – known I believe in Japan as 'the blossom for which the Emperor turned his carriage to look again'.

In Kyoto there is a temple where the cherry blossom seems to hang softly above the roofs of the red and green buildings, in contrast to the temple square with its white gravel reflecting the hard morning sun. Beyond the buildings is a garden, with walkways of weeping cherry, ponds with carp, and at their edge irises large and blue, with petals that tremble like exotic butterflies. There are, I suppose, far more cherry trees in Britain; it is just that the Japanese put them in the right places.

But for me the most wonderful sight is blossom like snow blowing from trees that grow on the banks of a canal. Even the trees themselves are worth looking at. Or rather, not so much the trees but the way they are wrapped and propped. Which gives them the strangest of shapes. They are propped, the Japanese say, to stop them blowing over in typhoons. Perhaps it is really to make them look better. They are wrapped in layers of straw matting. The idea is that the boring beetles which live in Japan will drill into the matting believing they have entered the tree, and lay their eggs between the mat and the tree, leaving the tree undamaged. I am inclined to believe that the Japanese just like wrapping things up.

The cherry blossom time is popular for weddings, with Sunday the most popular day. When I arrived at my hotel there were about twenty receptions going on at the same time. The brides were dressed in European white, the attendants wearing kimonos of the deepest plum. The bridegroom was dressed as I suppose Captain Pinkerton once dressed. Attendants carried great swathes of ghost orchids – the whole effect was very beautiful, but it seemed strange that all the grooms should dress in the same way, peculiar that all these brides should choose the same colour kimonos for the bridesmaids. Oh, how us travellers can misunderstand local customs. It was only later as I travelled in the lift that I noticed that these well-dressed grooms and bridesmaids were really the staff of the hotel in their uniforms, but then in Japan nothing is really how it seems.

Later, walking in the Ginza I saw in a shop window a painting by Yves Klein, beside it a sculpture by the same artist – both of museum quality. Believing this to be a gallery I went inside and found several gentlemen selling suits of the most conservative kind.

KEEPING NATURE IN TRIM

THE year had moved well into autumn as we know it before the leaves on the trees in Japan began to change colour, let alone fall from their trees. In the city of Kyoto the avenues of ginko trees had turned from green to yellow by the second week in November, but still they hung to the branches – their nuts having already fallen by this time. To pick up these much sought-after nuts, small boys dodge the early morning traffic, before they form orderly files to make their way to school. The ginko tree comes unchanged from prehistory, its split leaf an object of beauty used in Japanese cuisine both for decoration and also for eating. Round thin wafers are made with this leaf in the centre of them. The nuts are supposed to have a special power to increase the ability of the brain. They are quite expensive and in many Japanese households are locked away in a cupboard. Japanese men say to one another, 'Do not let the key of the cupboard where the nuts of the ginko tree are kept fall into the hands of women'. Having observed the attitudes of the Japanese male to his opposite sex, they are clearly frightened of anything that might change their status quo – even if it is only their wives and daughters having a surfeit of ginko nuts. The Japanese, being a particularly tidy race, are reluctant to let the leaves fall naturally from the trees that line their streets. Squads of them climb up ladders in November and pluck the leaves from the branches, stuffing them into large sacks supported from their waists.

There is a similar and equally extraordinary sight in Tokyo – gardeners are dangled on the ends of long ropes down the stone walls of the Imperial Palace, and then they pull off the ivy that grows there and put it in similar bags. These leaf pluckers work like demented squirrels, and their efforts have the trees suddenly bare. Then these men set about cutting the branches of the trees, making the whole thing into a shape pleasing to the eye. At this time of the year they do the same thing with the fir trees, cutting a branch here, a bundle of needles there. They work several men to a tree with certainty, never stepping back to have a look at how things are going. These arborial hairdressers seem to know what they are about, and the result is unusual, if not totally pleasing to the European eye.

We have a different approach to trees. For us, a tree must be large and full, the bigger the better. The trunk must be strong and have as great a diameter as possible, the branches sweeping almost to the ground. We like trees such as the oak, the beech, the horse chestnut. In evergreens, the giants among trees are the cedar and the wellingtonia. We secretly despise softwood – the firs of the Forestry Commission used to fill in useless land, the cherries in the streetscape of new towns and urban gardens. The Japanese greatly admire the cherry tree for its blossom, and the fir for its shape. We tend to leave trees alone until they get old and sick and then, if we prune them, it is to balance and retain the shape of their youth. They like that look old and twisted. They artificially change the shape of the tree by tying them down or propping them up and cutting bits off them. They are forever tinkering about with their trees.

I went to Japan that autumn to watch the leaves change colour; when it happens is largely dependent on how wet or dry the summer has been. The change takes about a week and a good place from which to watch it is Kyoto, a city surrounded by heavily wooded hills and, unlike some parts of America where all the woodlands change at the same time, and to just one colour from another, the change in Japan is slow and infinitely more subtle.

The woodland in Japan is made up of many different trees whose leaves change to different colours at different times. Each morning the view is different from the previous evening, and each evening different from that morning. The light changes during the day, reversing and speeding these changes. Almost every minute of the five days I spent in Kyoto this phenomenon was different. The ginko trees with their yellow leaves, the cherries' shades of bronze, the green firs, patches of bamboo forest yellow and green like flashes of lightning and the maples with their bright red leaves.

The Japanese are much taken with making things smaller. They have reproduced this grand landscape in miniature in the gardens of the Katsura Imperial Villa. The same compositions of colour are there – lakes, rivers and mountains have been built. It is the same landscape that surrounds the city of Kyoto. A great deal of trouble was taken over this garden 400 years ago and it has now been extremely well restored. The buildings are perfect, each in exactly the right position. But with its overhanging trees growing thick at the edge of the still and dirty water, it seemed to me terribly like a Surrey garden. Man at his best, even the Japanese, cannot compete with God: I am afraid the mistake that the creators of this garden made was not in competing with nature, but in having the natural product close at hand for comparison. The most beautiful of all the trees I saw the week I was there was the red maple, and of all the gardens that of Tofuku-Ji Temple, the Temple of Bubbling Springs. One of the best places to see these maples is the bridge between the two parts of that temple, a bridge built, legend has it, for the convenience of the monks, who were fed up with walking down one very steep slope and up another one to reach the spot where they say their prayers. However, it is my belief that they built the bridge just so they could see the trees better.

DAYS OF FAIRS AND ROSES

MAY is a bad month for collectors. It is the prelude to the antiques fair season, which opens in June, and dealers hold back choice items, hoping to make a bit of a splash at Grosvenor House (where the grandest and best of British fairs is held). A good display at the fair is supposed to interest the customer, but in fact the dealers do it only to impress each other. Collectors are not fond of queuing and struggling through a crowd. Rather than make a hasty decision while sweating under hot lights, most prefer to make a choice over a cup of tea in a dealer's back room, or, in the special case of the great Bond Street jeweller S. J. Phillips, over lunch and a bottle of Château-Lafite 1945. In May, the dealers stop dispensing tea, never mind wine. 'Come and see me at the fair,' they suggest.

I suspect the great days of the antiques fair are coming to an end. The costs of building the stands, moving the goods in and getting them out are bound to be reflected in the prices. Moreover, what bargains there are at a vast show such as the fair at London's Olympia are always snapped up by other dealers, who know where to find them long before their customers join the bunfight. Many serious collectors give that one a miss.

Yet it is difficult to escape them. There are fairs in Paris, New York and Amsterdam, and they are becoming a part of English country life. There is even an antiques fair in Hartley Wintney and when I visit it, for it is my local event, I think: 'Why can't antique dealers be dealers, not travelling salesmen?'

But May is not an absolute disaster. There are collections that can be added to only when the weather begins to improve: pre-Raphaelite churches, for instance. I have just discovered St Peter's in Scarborough, North Yorkshire, which is no place to seek out in inclement weather. But what most gladdens my heart in May is the appearance of old-fashioned roses, with names such as Buff Beauty, Félicité Perpétue, Princesse de Nassau, Vicomtesse Pierre de Fou, Fru Dagmar Hastrup, or that wonderful rugosa rose, *Rosa filipes* 'Kiftsgate', which grows 80 feet in a year when established; or its more manageable relative, Wedding Day. It is worth a journey to Kiftsgate just to see the *Rosa filipes* covering two fully grown copper beeches.

At Mottisfont Abbey, near Romsey, in Hampshire, a collection of more than 600 varieties of old roses has been put together by the master of this genre, Graham Stuart Thomas. They begin to bloom in May and end in July, the peak depending on the weather. At Mottisfont, the collection is laid out and labelled like a museum, and it is the inspiration for my rose collection.

As is the way with collections, the rose I want most is the one not at Mottisfont. It is called *Rosa chinensis*, and it is missing because it no longer survives in England. Small, red and almost insignificant, it is one of the four grandparents of all our English roses, and it scrambles over rocks in the gorges of the Yangtze River in China.

A few years ago, I went in search of a specimen, and I got to China all right. My expedition was at the right time of year, and I was able to organize a boat on the Yangtze. I have no complaints about the boat. It was a fine boat, and I'm sure the 1,200 other passengers enjoyed the trip immensely.

My cabin was comfortable, and the food delicious, the dockyards and panorama of Chinese industry were fascinating. The sporting facilities, viewed from the river, were not quite as attractive as Windsor racecourse seen from the Thames, though the comparison is not entirely fair. One of the delights of my youth was when my family took a picnic in a motor boat from Henley to Windsor.

My Chinese hosts were immensely kind, but there was no *Rosa chinensis*, or, if there was, I could not see it, and even if I had seen it, I had no means of getting to it. Somewhere, somehow, something had been lost in translation. All was not lost, however, for my Chinese hosts had got the idea that if I liked roses, I would like gardens.

How right they were, for they took me to Suzhou, where I saw 12 gardens – too many and too fine to describe here. But one, the Humble Administrator's Garden, must receive mention. He was an ancient Chancellor of the Exchequer, torn from power because of failure to balance the budget, perhaps. He whittled away his enforced retirement by creating the most beautiful garden in the world.

The true mystery of this garden lies in the fact that there are very few flowers in it. It is less than two acres, and it is composed mostly of buildings and water, bridges and pavilions. There are also occasional shrubs, and trees that are twisted and stunted, all carefully manicured by the gardeners. Nature has been shaped to fit. It is paradise delineated by moon gates and pagodas.

The humble administrator died just as the garden was completed. This was fitting, because he had achieved perfection. There was no more to do; had he lived, his life would have been so empty that he must have died of heartbreak.

I never found my rose in China, though I still hope that I may one day add it to my collection. The more I think about it, the more convinced I become that the idea of an object is greatly more important than the object itself.

LIVE AND LET THAI

BANGKOK is a name that seems to indicate that the capital of Thailand is as exotic a place as you could wish to visit. At Bangkok airport there are palm trees and orchids, and queues seem to be a speciality as well. Not because there is a rush by the travellers of the world to visit the place, but rather because the young lady who deals with immigration papers takes an average of four minutes per visitor. The Thais have a reputation for friendliness, and their immigration officials excel in this respect. They laugh and talk to each other all the while they puzzle over the complicated forms devised by their superiors. There are at this airport nearly sixty desks all with officials who deal with such matters. But there are still queues that make the crowds at the opening day of the Harrod's sale seem sparse.

Hot from waiting, hot from the traffic on the drive into the city and tired from travel and dust, the hotel seemed paradise. Green gardens touched with bougainvillaea, a blue pool and the river beyond – in the foyer of this hotel stylish Italians lazed in the giant armchairs. An hour or two there and this paradise changed; the stylish Italians became sluggish Germans. The pool appeared much smaller, the river dirty. This hotel, to my mind, had become just another example of concrete and greenery decorated with elements of the Orient – elements so distorted as to lose the beauty that they once had. It had become in fact the sort of hotel that you find from Honolulu to Singapore.

Motor boats race up and down this dirty river, long narrow boats, their prows high in the air with bunches of plastic orchids hanging from them, their sterns weighed down by an aircraft engine mounted about chest-height and driving a propeller at the end of a long piece of pipe. The driver lifts this propeller in or out of the water as he will. He turns it to the right or the left, spewing oil into the river and fumes into the air.

The canals have changed considerably over the years. The people who used to live there have largely left. Why should people live in cramped conditions over rat-infested water using only the most primitive forms of sanitation, just because it looks attractive for the tourists? Anyway tourists are there in plenty. The canals that remain have become a parade of motor boats ploughing their way through oil. The floating market seems to have moved to the land – leaving in its place a giant traffic jam of motor launches.

The houses have mostly been demolished, and only the rotting stumps that were their foundations remain. To stop the erosion great lengths of the canal banks have been piled – steel sheet piles that somehow do not really have the same feel of the Orient about them that the timber houses had, although it's true that the occasional floating refreshment stall is still to be found. These dwellers of the waterways, who in their youth played in the water of the canals among the ducks and the waterlilies, are now grown and have removed themselves to flats nearby – concrete blocks built in the last few years. It is really amazing what the Orient can do to concrete, a material which in our climate seems harder than rock, but once it gets anywhere near the equator seems to rot, crumbling away and leaving steel bars exposed which in time turn to rust, and then the concrete crumbles again.

On the banks of these canals there are occasional temples and their monks. The last part of our century seems to have attacked these temples, for lurid signs made with fluorescent tube announce whatever message was once painted on boards. These once beautiful buildings have been crudely altered. On another canal there is the crocodile farm and of course the snake farm complete with a row of concrete men wrestling with concrete snakes, men and snakes painted in frightening colours. Apart from the snakes, the crocodiles and the temples there is little to see, and if you had the good fortune to travel these canals in the past then there is a great deal to mourn.

On the banks of Bangkok's main river there is a building called River City. Four floors of wall-to-wall shopping. The third and fourth floors are given over to antique shops such as 'The Great Dragon', whose sign goes on to inform the curious that its contents are 'the ultimate expression of your good taste'. I looked inside and thought about this notice. I am bound to say it puzzled me a little. Another shop, 'Thai Foundry', announced that it 'casts your bronzes better'. I could see that. The bronzes for sale had indeed been very well cast but why they had been cast eluded me entirely.

Neither of these shops, however, had prepared me for the shock of 'Chieng Heng Collection Co Ltd'. The horses for a start, horses of all periods and for that matter nearly all sizes – some far greater than life size. Horses standing, laying, rolling and rearing – all cast

Get stuffed

in bronze. But if you are not keen on horses, then they had bronze hippoptamuses, zebras, the greater kudu and leopards, not to mention grizzly bears and swans – every sort of animal in fact. The warrior department held examples of bronze warriors mythological and historical – from Perseus to King Richard I. Medieval knights to the warriors of Genghis Khan and latter-day Arab warriors – one on a horse. But among all of these one piece stood out: a giant bronze budgerigar six or seven feet tall with a bright red beak.

Bangkok claims to be a city of a thousand canals – the Venice of the east? Never!

STREET IN SINGAPORE

A FLIGHT to Australia is a long and tedious affair which I thought could be eased by three days in Singapore to break the boredom. After leaving its mega-airport – a labyrinth of moving stairways, fresh-decked with fluorescent orchids, like some Eastern shrine to the modern world – the traveller encounters, on each side of the road into town, rows of hibiscus, rows of lilies. In fact, serried ranks of tropical plants that seem at first enchanting then monotonous – vast quantities of trees and plants, but of only half-a-dozen varieties.

Singapore is a difficult city to arrive at for there are so many trees in the city that it seems like the countryside and so many buildings in the countryside that it seems like the city. No smell of exotic perfume here, no smell of oriental spice, just petrol. Its now expensive aroma hangs in the hot and sweaty air, kept captive by banks of cloud, washed almost daily by heavy rain. It is a good rule of thumb that if a country has a large quantity of lush greenery it always gets a large quantity of rain. There is a monotony about Singapore found, I believe, nowhere else. The shops – Chanel, Cartier, Louis Vuitton, not one, but multiple agencies of these great houses – selling their products half a season behind the rest of the world. Twelve hours by aeroplane from winter to summer, but in Singapore it is hard to tell one from the other. Seasons here become irrelevant and so the fashions in these fashionable shops trail behind, unsold goods lingering on the shelves.

Singapore's buildings, built with all the advantages of blatant commerce, have failed – towers, scaled down from other towns, clippings from architectural magazines pasted into this city then hidden with trailing bougainvillaea and filled with potted palms. The high-ceilinged foyers of the early 1960s with their overgrown chandeliers of cascading glass. New buildings that were once Singapore's pride now seem like a reproach. Systematically they have, for nearly 25 years, destroyed everything that was old. Hotels everywhere, snatched from any American city and built in Singapore, everywhere there are orchids – in every foyer, in every room, on every table, tucked in napkins on trays, delivered with the morning papers – there is nowhere to go, nothing to do, that does not involve orchids, and always the same sort of orchid.

To be fair to Singapore – a city that offers no real reason to be fair to it – the mood has changed. They are now rebuilding the old buildings as quickly as they can. Chinese merchants and Malay traders are being moved back into reproductions of the shops that they occupied before they were decanted into modern blocks. Bugis Street is being rebuilt – rebuilt somewhere else, for its original site is now the headquarters of the Urban Transit Authority. The Tourist Authority feel the need to recreate some local colour and no doubt a Bugis Street Authority will be created to do just this. The days when you had to kick the pipes in Raffles Hotel to start the flow of water are long gone. The days of the old Bugis Street – a street closed to traffic, opened to food, and the world's greatest form of theatre: the accident of large numbers of people enjoying themselves. Tables all over the pavement, tables all over the street. Food that crosses the borders of the Far East. Nothing that you could not buy in that street, nothing, I suppose, that you could not sell. Packed with travellers, drinking, eating, laughing and, very much later, tears and fights. The nightly parade of transvestites, quite beautiful in their way, posing for photographs with the diners, poking fun at drunks who perhaps did not realize that the beautiful girl they hugged had more to her. A visit to Bugis Street was an event. Nothing really to do with the buildings, it was about people – not special people, but special I suppose because of their ordinariness. A drunken sailor standing on a table pouring beer over himself, a party of Australians, the most ungainly of travellers. How can you rebuild this? Better let it go.

To wake after the flight that night and to look down on the blue fingers of Sydney Harbour, its white Opera House and grey steel bridge, a city of clean air, a dry city with roofs poking like red pimples through its greenery, a sight that caused some great figure visiting from Europe to exclaim to the press at the airport: 'My first impression of Sydney ^ impetigo'.

Impetus "on the move" going forward

SIX

PEARLS FROM OZ

WORTH GIVING A XXXX FOR

AUSTRALIA is the new continent, and its people are so direct they make Americans appear genteel. It is not, on the face of it, a promising place for collectors. But the reverse is true. Two of my choicest collections are to be found there. They consist of the work of man and of nature, and combine to form a culture unique to this continent. But before elaborating, let me dispose of some of the more familiar Australian collections that I am not talking about here.

Australiana, for instance. This means acquiring an object – any object – that has a kangaroo or an emu on it: jugs, tins, odds and ends. This is not collecting, it is accumulating. Nor do I mean aboriginal art, though a several-thousand-year-old tradition has produced objects that range from the incredibly beautiful to the mundane. I do not even mean the great painters, like Arthur Streeton of the 19th century, or the 20th-century Australian masters, Sidney Nolan and Arthur Boyd.

The first of the collections that I admire was put together by God, and I am thinking of the big pieces, not of the smaller natural objects – the incredible range of shells on the coastline; the amazing fossils, sometimes opalized to produce objects that would do credit to a Renaissance court jeweller; the birds; and the pearls of unequalled size and lustre. This collection contains no objects that can be held in the hand or placed in a cabinet.

I am thinking of the great masterpieces of nature that enrich this country; of the scale of the Simpson desert and the waterfalls on the Prince Regent River; of the rock, carved by the wind and rain to the shape of a great red sleeping dog, called Ayers Rock but now in the style of correctness, named Uluru ; and of Bungle Bungle, the recently discovered domes, rising from the earth and ringed round with bright red hanging gardens caught like a papal crown in its crevasses.

In the gorges of the Kimberleys you stand alone yet always sense someone else's presence – it could be an aboriginal behind the bush, or God: you take your pick. In the Wittenoom gorges in the Hammersley Range are high rock faces that leave an impression to compare with Indian temples or Gothic cathedrals.

These works of art were created by the heaving of the seabed and the chiselling of the wind. The collector stands in awe of their greatness and wonders whether any gilt-framed canvas will ever seem the same again; whether any man can reproduce such great beauty. Reproductions, like the memory, are false.

The photographs in tourist brochures are delightful but they fail to tell the truth about this hard land in northern Australia, where drought and famine are common and there is seldom a feast. There is either no rain or too much; when rivers flood, water spreads for hundreds of miles. It is a beautiful but inhospitable place. For the first white men to cross the continent, coping with the land meant cheating death. Adaptation to this primitive environment started a new cultural tradition, known as first settlement furniture. Made in the bush by the early settlers, its forms were dictated by the harsness of nature, yet owe little to it.

I have a chest of drawers made from wooden boxes formerly used to transport cans of oil. Shell Oil's mollusc is emblazoned on the face of each drawer. It is stained green and the effect is delightful. Another piece is a chair; the seat is an orange box and the legs are sticks. Its companion is a slab of red gum supported by the axle spring from a wagon. There are tables made from Jarrah wood, and cupboards made in optimistic imitation of the European counterparts, with the trade stencil still showing clearly on the timber. Men and women living here under barely tolerable conditions enriched their lives by adding decoration to their furniture in the bush. Despite the daily struggle for survival, these people had an eye for beauty and design – and used it.

As settlers moved across the continent, they took with them the memories of home. English, Welsh, Scottish and Irish techniques of cabinet-making, based on remembered styles from the century before, married with later-arrived German and French traditions to produce one of the most virile and least collected genres in the history of furniture-making. Since this is the kind of furniture that gets thrown away when there is enough money for a new three-piece suite, or when the children come to clear the family farm, there is not much of it to be found and the stock is diminishing. A few dealers in Sydney have begun to appreciate its worth, but the museums have yet truly to do so. One day they will.

What have we learned? That great beauty exists not only in a remarkable variety of forms but also in places that seem to be most unpromising.

OUTBACK ARTISTS ARE IN

TRAVELLING in Australia, or rather urban Australia, which is where 90 per cent of the people live, I am struck by the interest in art – not art in general, but Australian art, particularly 19th- and 20th-century Australian painting in the European idiom. There is hardly a restaurant in Melbourne or Sydney that doesn't hang works by Australian painters. Certainly, no bank is without a 20th-century Australian painting or sculpture in its foyer, or a 19th-century Australian painting in the boardroom. The art of France, America, Britain, not to mention Spain, Italy and the rest of Europe, has no place here. The names of the great icons that we admire – Picasso, Matisse, Bacon, Moore – are to be found in museums, but not in houses, office buildings or banking halls. Australians collect Australian art.

Their first artists were visitors from other countries, recording the plants and animals of Australia, to show to an astonished world what a kangaroo looked like. Convict painters first recorded life in the colonies or, in the case of William Buelow Gould, death in the colonies: heaps of dead game and fish, carefully reproduced, complete with blow flies. The first serious school of Australian painting was located in the bush not far from Melbourne at a place called Box Hill, where three painters named Roberts, M'Cubbin and Abrahams lived in the 1880s. They painted in the style of the French impressionists.

For reasons of economy, they painted on empty cigar boxes. Abrahams's father was an importer of cigars. (He was, incidentally, also grandfather to Sir Denys Lasdun, the National Theatre's architect.) In 1889 this group of painters held an exhibition that was called 9" × 5" Impressions – nine inches by five being the size of a cigar-box lid. (Australians were clearly not smoking Larranaga Magnums which come in a somewhat larger box.) These antipodean impressionists – whose most recent exhibition was called Golden Summers – drew a mist of happiness over their harsh and dangerous landscape. Their work is in vogue and fetches great sums.

Australian painting trundled along, without arousing much interest among European collectors until the Second World War, when a group called the Angry Penguins emerged. These were painters and writers whose trumpet was a magazine by that name, and who were fighting one of the obscure battles that seem to obsess the art world but which have no relevance for the collector. The argument was explained in detail in the catalogue produced for the stunning exhibition of the Angry Penguins' work that opened at the Hayward Gallery in May that year, and subsequently moved to the Tate Gallery's Liverpool branch. By this time several artists were painting the Australian outback, but none caught the reality of the bush in the way Sir Sydney Nolan first did in the early 1940s.

Nolan's bush strikes fear into the urban population of Australia. I don't refer to the bush near Sydney or Melbourne, Perth or Adelaide, which I call the Sunday Bush. I am thinking of the deserts of central Australia, the jungle of Arnhem Land, the windswept bush of the Gulf of Carpentaria and the arid uplands of the Kimberlies – country where death by dehydration can come on you in a five-mile walk from a broken-down vehicle. This is the bush where no one asks another where a man is from, or where he goes, where laughter is crude and unforgiving and violence equates with humour, where a joke can be made of death.

The landscape predates man, and the bush has resisted almost every attempt by Europeans to destroy it. It has resisted cattle, sheep, mining, litter, and even demand for Aboriginal bark paintings. This is the hard bush, and Nolan paints it as it is. The rest paint it as they imagine it to be from the comfort of a Sydney drawing room.

Arthur Boyd put strength, not into the landscapes, but into his figures – savage birds, and beasts, and bulls. Russell Drysdale paints soft landscapes with strong people. John Olsen's bush is lonely and distorted, empty but full of humour. John Percival painted Demented Swans (no kidding). As is the fashion, there is also a mass of painters working in the modern idiom, from Brett Whitely down, or on. Slowly, the styles of the painters in European idiom and those of the indigenous people merge. This is art that is conscious of Australia's proximity to the Far East.

Art in Australia takes two paths. There are paintings about the country as a place, and as a nation. There is freshness in the sunshine, the people, the cities and in the paintings, whether they are good or bad. If you are excited about Australia, you will be excited about its art. I suspect this strange continent makes collectors of pictures. In Sydney, the doyen of the dealers is Barry Stern, whose exquisite and catholic tastes make his gallery a good place to start. Melbourne dealers say the market is booming. A Sydney dealer told me bright colours are selling well; Queenslanders like bright pictures. In Perth the market is red hot. In Adelaide they lectured me on the mathematics of differential pricing. I search the Australian art market for a gem. I found a mass of paintings I liked. The only thing the dealers haven't got is a sense of humour. They still tell jokes in Cork Street. In the southern hemisphere collecting art is a serious business.

IN DEFENCE OF DEALERS

ART dealers are thought of a shady characters at best, but likely to be downright charlatans, ranking in public esteem a little above criminals and politicians. This negative view has a profound effect on the way the customers view the trade. It is amazing, the way they feel that a dealer is obliged to give them a bargain when they buy a picture. Yet they do not feel a similar obligation to pay, delaying settlement for months on the assumption that the dealer probably made too big a profit on the deal. They ignore the fact that dealers in art are no different from motor manufacturers when it comes to covering the costs of the business.

Worse still, if the artist's work has failed to prosper, the customer often returns the painting to the gallery, usually in a large car, driven by the chauffeur, along with a complicated message about changing the colour of the dining-room walls and a request for the refunding of the £200 paid two years earlier. The message ends with the news that the chauffeur will wait for the cheque.

In this hostile environment dealers soon discover that, no matter how competitive the business, they need each other – a self-evident truth brought home to me most recently at a Shinju Matsuri festival in Broome, Western Australia, late in August. This is the festival of the pearl, celebrating the end of the harvest when the luggers laid up for the summer break. It is multinational, with Malays, Japanese, Chinese as well as European Australians, plus the Aboriginals who preceeded them all.

The market that accompanies the fair is like markets that accompany fairs wherever they take place, and one of the dealers with a stand there is a young lad of Aboriginal descent, smart, with broad feet and narrow pointed shoes, imported from Italy. His sales technique is lent a certain urgency by his discomfort. This year he had the idea of selling what he called 'real Chinese jade'.

The Chinese community in Broome is prominent, and after conferring with his colleagues, a respected member of the community shuffled up to the Aboriginal lad. He pointed to the jade and said: 'This one Kimberly coloured stone.' As he did so, the crowd melted away.

As the Chinese went back to his group, the lad ran after him and seized him by the shoulder. While the Chinese closed ranks, he shouted: 'Listen, do I tell people what you put in your long soup?'

Then he walked off with as much of a stride as his shoes would allow. Having considered the situation, the Chinese shuffled back to the stand, and, striking an inscrutable pose, announced: 'This is pure Chinese jade. Absolutely pure.'

What he knew, and the lad knew, but the crowd did not, is that the secret ingredients in his long soup is Actifed syrup, which also serves as a well-known international cough mixture. The world being the way it is, they had reached a necessary accommodation with each other.

Despite this, and other tales of the saleroom, I have trusted art dealers. One or two have stretched the truth, but, by and large, it is a world in which honesty prospers and dishonesty gets its just reward in the end. When I was collecting American abstract expressionist paintings in the early 1960s, I put myself in the hands of Leslie Waddington, the owner of the Waddington Galleries. Friends described me as quite mad, but he helped me build an important collection of painting and sculpture, and when events dictated that they be sold, his help was invaluable. Dealers and collectors are actually good for each other, for the combination of professionalism and enthusiasm is formidable.

But there are occasions on which even the shrewdest dealers can be of no help to the most inspired collector. This is the second truth I recalled this summer.

Further up the Australian coastline from Broome lies Darwin. This beautiful tropical city is the headquarters of Nick Paspaley, Australia's leading pearling master. I watched this year's crop being sorted. There was a small mountain of pearls ranging in colour from steel grey, through gold in all its shades to white and palest pink. There were baroque pearls and tear drops, button pearls and perfectly round ones; literally sacks of them.

Then Paspaley asked if I would like to see a few pearls that he had put on one side. He drew a bag from the safe and spilled the pearls on a velvet tray. The quality was truly incredible. 'Each of these pearls I have picked because I have never seen its like before,' he said.

One specimen brought to mind the parable of the pearl of great price (St Matthew, Chapter 13, you will recall). I have always known that feeling: finding something for which I would sell everything. It is the symptom by which a true collector can be recognized. This pearl was pear shaped, 15 millimetres in diameter and Nick Paspaley called its colour strawberry, but to me it appeared at first to be coloured pale gold, and then changed before my eyes to pale pink. Every time I moved it between my fingers, the colour changed. I asked if I could buy it.

Paspaley took it, looked it over and slipped it back into its bag before returning it to his safe. 'How can you price a pearl like this? This pearl has no price,' he said.

No price; no deal.

GREED AND GOOD TASTE

THIS is a dealer's tale. She was keen, young, with a nicely turned ankle and immaculate grammar. When she came across a fine painting, it was not by chance, for it was her trade. One day she sought out a 19th-century picture of horse racing in South Australia. It was not a picture that would become the subject of a scholarly article by Denys Sutton in *Apollo*, nor would it find itself on the pages of the *Burlington Magazine*, but for a collector whose taste runs more to horses than painting, and who lives in Australia, it was, after its fashion, a masterpiece. It was a painting with a ready market among the wealthy of New South Wales. But that made it a one-hit picture: fail with it in Australia and it is yours for life, for it will surely remain there in stock to worry your heirs.

Our dealer hesitated. Maybe it was natural caution, but she struck no deal. She did not buy the picture but she did acquire a photograph and reached an understanding with the owner. Our dealer would journey to Australia and offer the painting to a client. Not, I must add, a client known personally to the dealer, but a collector on such a grand scale that he retains his own agent who cares about details like authenticity and provenance.

By chance or intent – we shall never know for sure – this agent was bypassed, and an appointment made with the grand client. Australia is a long way by anyone's standards, and, as the miles passed in the dark unsleeping hours of a night flight, the beauty of the painting had grown in the mind of our dealer. So had the price. The photograph was shown to the client and a price of 225,000 asked for.

'You mean dollars, my dear?' said the client.

'Pounds,' she replied. 'Not a penny less,' she added, echoing the words of Jeffrey Archer.

'Such a price,' said the client. 'Impossible.'

'But such a picture,' she replied. 'So early for Australia. It is so rare ... such a chance ... there are, of course, many other distinguished collectors ... came to you first ... admire your taste, acumen, judgement.' She deployed all the blandishments of her trade; all the flattery that turns a bicycle's handle bars into a Picasso. Having finished her recital, she returned the photograph to its envelope. But, as she made to go, the client asked to see the photograph again.

He returned it to her once more. 'My dear,' he said, 'I'm afriad I have bad news for you.'

'But the painting is of great quality,' she said, thinking that he did not admire it.

'Indeed. Any 10 collectors would have this painting in the rustling of a cheque. The painting is all that you say it is, perhaps even more. No, my dear, the bad news is that I acquired the work last week.'

'Impossible,' she gasped.

'No, my dear, quite possible. And only £125,000.'

The moral: that you mustn't sell what you do not own.

Every collector whose greed has sprung a dealer's careful trap may squeal with delight at this story. Every young lad who bought a silver dish or piece of porcelain that is not quite what it purported to be on the day of purchase may celebrate in the knowledge of a dealer caught.

Or pause, and weep, for the great dealer – and this dealer may one day be great – is the friend of the collector. Through this friendship, the dealer becomes the collector's other half, his twin in collecting, as keen to form a collection as the collector. Use such a dealer. The young lady's mistake was not the price she asked, which showed courage. Her mistake was the caution she revealed in not buying the painting in the first place. A dealer's profit is a payment for skill. In this case, our young dealer did not display sufficient skill and lost her profit.

Among many strange beliefs held by even the most sophisticated of peoples is the one embraced by London dealers that the newly rich of Australia are an easy mark – kookaburras there to be plucked. This belief seems to lack logic, for if a man has just made a large amount of money through his skill and shrewdness, he will surely be among the hardest of people to take money from. Nevertheless, stories abound concerning both these tycoons and the optimistic dealers of London.

This is the story of three men: a great prince, a tycoon, and a London dealer known for the touching honesty with which he restores furniture. He is a man who scrapes every vestige of the kindness of time from a piece of furniture and returns it faithfully to its bright new condition. Now this man had a prince among tables in his possession. A table fit for a prince, and when a large slice of the wealth of Australia walked in and inquired about the price, it was only a moment before a deal was struck.

A night or two later, the dealer dined with a real prince, who mentioned, as I suppose princes do, that he required various fine pieces of furniture, among them a table. He was a prince; the dealer had a princely table. The deal was struck again. The table was delivered to the prince, and the Australian's cheque was returned. After all, a peasant must give way to a prince.

This, however, is not how Australian peasants see these matters. Lawyers were called. There was acrimony: to sue or not to sue. The dealer was confident: an Australian would not have the temerity to sue a prince, surely? The Australian viewed this matter with refreshing clarity and I dined at this table, perhaps a king among tables, in Australia, where it is now settled.

The moral of this tale is that antiques can be sold only once, or, rather, to only one customer at a time, regardless of the temptations of the second offer. When an object you owned is sold and sold again for ever-increasing sums, don't think about it. The important price is the one that was paid to you. As for the profit that accrues to others, smile and take pleasure in the evidence of your own good taste.

THE WISDOM OF OZ

THE momentous events in Eastern Europe and the black comedy of people collecting lumps of the Berlin Wall, the current boom in the salerooms with recorded prices for paintings smashed every week, seemed very remote to me as I walked down Cable Beach in Broome, the most north-west point of Australia, where people collect old bottles and very remarkable sea shells from the water instead. The first overland telegraph came ashore at Broome. The only bank robbery in the town's history was carried out by a man on a bicycle, and the fire station burned to the ground because the fireman could not get into the station to get out the fire engine. The smell is of frangipanis and tropical blooms in the town, and the sea and the bush along the fifteen-mile beach. The main tourist attraction is the Japanese graveyard where generations of pearl divers are buried, most of them killed in the course of their work. Pearls, diamonds and cattle are found here, and it is one of the world's last great unexplored wildernesses.

Early most mornings, I walked down the beach with a man who, in the vernacular, would be described as 'my mate Snowy'. He is a pearling master, or rather the owner of a farm that produces the very large and beautiful pearls that are sometimes seen around the necks of the world's most beautiful women (for that is how they seem when they are wearing them), round pearls of gem quality. But for every 1000 pearls produced, there are only two or three that the pearling master will describe as 'super' whether they be baroque, or grey, or pink, or golden, or white with a deep deep lustre, and no super pearl is smaller than ten millimetres in diameter, the largest the size of a damson.

'My mate Snowy' makes Crocodile Dundee look like a West End car salesman, and some years ago when he was starting his pearl farm, he regularly drove the three hours down the track for supplies. On one occasion the back of the truck was full of cardboard boxes containing plastic baskets and sitting beside him was a young Japanese diver who was chainsmoking and casting the cigarette butts out of the window.

'It's hot today,' Snowy remarked.

'Very hot,' replied the diver taking off his shirt.

'Bloody hot,' said Snowy taking off his shirt as well.

'Very, very hot,' replied the Japanese, taking off his trousers.

Now Snowy is used to hot weather but, before long, both he and the diver were bumping along in their underpants.

It was a rough track (in fact it may be misleading even to describe it as a track). Snowy slowed as he approached a particularly deep ditch, and to his surprise the cab was engulfed in a sheet of flame. The pair of them jumped out and ran into the bush – or rather what was left of the bush after a fire the previous week. Snowy explained to the diver in language that tended towards the crude that it is not a good idea to throw lighted cigarettes out of a moving vehicle, as the truck exploded.

Having got that off his chest, Snowy addressed the problem, which was that they were fifteen miles from their camp on a road that only they used, with no water, no hats, no shoes and only two pairs of underpants between them. Snowy took off his pants, tore them into strips and tied them to his feet. The diver did the same and they began to trudge through the bush. The temperature was forty-six degrees centigrade, and after five miles the diver lay down in a salt pan to die – Snowy's best efforts couldn't move him. So Snowy walked on, sometimes over rocks that were so hot that you could fry eggs on them – and then grill the bacon in their reflected heat.

Eventually, Snowy reached the camp, put his head in a water trough and then called for help: 'There's a bloke out there on his back in a salt pan. Throw some water on him and bring him in.' Nothing could make the price of a van Gogh seem more irrelevant.

SHELL COMPANY

MY first shell collection came from the beach at Bournemouth. Like other little boys, I found these pretty, useless objects irresistible and took them, covered in sand in a plastic bucket, back to the hotel and washed them in a basin, to the distress, I suppose, of the maids.

I began my second collection walking each morning along Cable Beach, an incredible 15-mile strip of sand that starts at Broome in Western Australia, where I spend some time. Cable Beach is uncluttered by surf boards or beach umbrellas. The air is fresh with the smell of bush plants growing in the dunes. Sea eagles coast above the beach and migratory wading birds that, like me, have flown in from northern Europe, rise in clouds from the gentle surf. The sea is a highway for migrating whales and a resort for turtles and dolphins; on the beach, phalanxes of sea shells glistening colourfully in the sun. I cannot resist it.

But life for the adult collector is not as easy, I'm afraid, as for little boys. Shells gather in the early morning quickly dry out on the breakfast table. As if cursed by an appalling mystical force, they become dull and lifeless, like the ones I collected in Bournemouth and despised when they lost their lustre.

The glistening gems accumulated by true shell collectors have to be plucked from a reef deep in the ocean or dredged from its bottom. Then, when the inhabitant of this strangely shaped skin is removed, time stops for the shell and its lustre is preserved for ever in its pristine state in readiness to join a collection.

Collectors, however, must beware the little-known phenomenon of the killer sea shell. Some of the cone shells – *Conus textile* and *Conus striatus*, for instance – are among the nine or so varieties that sometimes fight back. These are violent creatures, fish-eating shells that shoot a small dart of poison into their victims. Paralysis and death follow, suggesting that it can be deeply unwise to look down the wrong end of a loaded cone shell.

In Australia, paralysis and death are not the only fates that can befall unwary shell collectors. Large areas of the coastline are national parks, and collectors caught plundering the shells are subject to heavy fines. Moreover, a licence is needed to export Australian flora or fauna, and to smuggle out specimens can bring a fine of up to A$100,000.

I recently observed the law in action at Perth airport. A seemingly innocent man with a scruffy leather case was queuing to check in his luggage with Qantas when a hand fell on his shoulder and voice ordered him to open the case. The tones brooked no doubt that the man was a criminal. So he was, for inside his case were at least 50 parrots, each with its head and tail sticking out of a cardboard tube.

How was he spotted? I asked the Qantas clerk. 'Somebody squawked,' he replied drily.

No laws prevented the early explorers of the southern hemisphere, such as William Dampier and Captain Cook, from bringing excellent examples of Australian shells to Europe, where they were mounted on silver or gold. Indeed, they have a place in history: primitive people used them for dress, and Pocahontas, the American Indian princess who befriended the early settlers, wore them as wampum. The nautilus shell is the image of the renaissance, and Hawaiians used the golden cowrie as a symbol of royalty. Cowrie shells have surfaces so smooth and a texture so perfect that they are called porcelain by the French, and they are the pride of any shell collector's cabinet. (As stamps are kept in albums, shells are kept in cabinets.)

As in all forms of collecting, shell specialists have their eccentricities. Some collect freaks – misshapen or miscoloured shells – cones, spiked shells or white shells. Some collect giant clams, others cowries so small that they can be observed only under a magnifying glass and picked up with tweezers. Collectors of Victoriana prize particularly the pretty shells arranged in patterns in boxes made by seamen on long and lonely voyages.

The sums of money that pass between a dealer and a collector are considerable.

Of course, primitive people also used shells for money – the *Cowrie moneta* was one of the earliest forms of currency – so perhaps shells are money after all. Perhaps that is why people collect them.

Down but not Under

Perth in Western Australia, a state the size of Western Europe, is the most isolated city in the world – nothing much but desert lies between it and most of Australia's population in the south-east. Nearly 35 years have past since I first visited the city, arriving by ship at the port of Fremantle. The great liner's docks were crowded with migrants; migrants who had left so little and arrived to expect so much, their white skins burned red by the Indian Ocean's sun. They walked towards the immigration officers, seated behind desks, their children dragged by the arm as they looked around, children carrying their world in a basket. A lone piper stood and played as the passengers came ashore. This was Australia, the lucky country, where now the luck has run out. The 'golden west', that is what these people had been told by those paid to persuade them to travel there free. The Cinderella state, that is what those who lived and worked there called Western Australia. But Cinderella did go to the ball, and what a ball that 35 years has been.

In those days Perth was barely a city, more like a big farming

This is the way it used to be, before we got lucky.

town – you expected to see cattle and drovers in the main street, an elegant street, with buildings of the 1930s seldom more than three or four storeys high, built in the soft yellow Doneybrook stone not unlike that of Bath. Offices were fitted out with the dark-brown jarrah wood, grown in the south of the state, taken from trees that grow several hundred feet high. At the end of Perth's elegant and comfortable main street stood a fortress known as the Barracks, a fortress that looked for all the world like a child's toy castle. In those days, you never saw a policeman; crime was, a citizen of Perth might say, 'rare as hen's teeth'. If you saw a girl standing on a street corner late at night (and you often did), she was there waiting for a bus, and at night the buses ran at long intervals.

The best restaurant was called Luis, and it is still there. In those days it was decorated with printed colour reproductions of the great paintings by Degas, Monet and Renoir – 'I am told that these pictures,' said my host, 'are extremely valuable'. The food was awful and, like the pictures, imitation – the proprietor of Luis knew little about French art or cooking. The citizens in those days all seemed to be big men, well over six feet tall, with heads like shopping baskets and hands like shovels – their faces burned brown. They wore grey suits and brown fedora hats, looking at you from under wide brims that made no attempt to hide their eyes. Then things began to change in the 1980s, the movers and shakers took over from the tall men; they were short and fat, with bald heads, and if they wore a hat, it was a yachting cap. Their suits were blue, too bright a blue, with too much silken thread in the weave – shiny men. The America's Cup came and Perth became a party, the state changed the slogan on its car number plates from 'The Wild Flower State' to 'The State of Excitement'. A small city, the whole world now knew about Perth. That is where the tycoons come from, that is where the deals are done.

In the old days, the Swan river flowed at the very edge of the town, but the planners soon fixed that. They filled in its peaceful bays and built a motorway that curls like a tortured snake, and to ease the pain of this motorway they planted gardens in between its coils, with little bridges and little ponds, and then a grateful government gave the planner who did all this the Order of Australia. Where once the architects of West Australia benefited from their isolation and built small new buildings in scale with their town, they now started to read the glossy architectural magazines and build glossy buildings and, like the proprietor of Luis Restaurant, they could not get it quite right. Now in the depths of recession the emptiness of these buildings stares through shiny glass that once reflected the greed of the men who owned them. Their concrete piazzas, empty of people, have concrete pots and windswept trees – the main street, once-beautiful St George Terrace, is a wind-filled canyon and the toy castle gone.

The luck seems to have gone as well, but Australia is built on bankruptcy, with an endless supply of optimistic Australians waiting to take over where others failed, and nowhere more than in Western Australia, for the west is a hard country and her people hardened by her; as fast as a shop fails, a restaurant or café opens. The whole population seem to have given up shopping and taken up eating. There can be nowhere with so few people and so many restaurants. Not the plush paint and velour of the past, these new places are decorated with whatever comes to hand, and all the better for it. This city, for all its changes, again has the feel of the 1960s; the citizens still play bowls dressed in their whites, the peppermint trees still stand in the suburb of Peppermint Grove. The lucky country? Oscar Wilde said, 'Success is entirely due to luck, ask any failure.' The people of Western Australia are learning that the ball is over – Cinderella is back in the kitchen and luck comes only with effort.

SEVEN

COLLECTING PAN-AMERICA

FIRST BITE AT THE BIG APPLE

I FIRST visited New York in 1956 travelling on *The Queen Elizabeth* – the old *Queen Elizabeth* that is. Travel for first-class passengers on this ship was a luxurious affair. Dinner-jackets were worn every night except for the evening we left, and dinner for those who know about travel was taken in the Verandah Grill. Passengers booked their table at the same time as they booked their tickets, for tables were hard to obtain: the Grill was smaller than the restaurant and the food was believed to be better. Besides, it was *the* place to eat and it seemed to me as a small boy that all the grand people there in couture clothes and jewellery with massive stones ate little other than caviar.

Then there was a ship's photographer determined to record every mouthful consumed. I travelled with my family. My mother hated the flash of cameras and took an intense dislike to this photographer. 'Please ask him not photograph us,' she requested. My father became desperate, for the man was insistent – with some reason, I suppose, for it was his job to take everyone's photograph and everyone except my mother was only too keen to have it taken. (This I might say was not the only respect in which my mother was unusual.) There seemed nothing that would stop the man; desperate measures were called for. 'Look – I'm not with my wife, I cannot be photographed,' shouted my father. This threw the photographer, and meant that my mother, father, grandmother and her aged female companion, my ten-year-old younger brother, my older brother and an aunt who travelled with us were able to enjoy our dinner unphotographed for the next four days. My father was pursued by the photographer trying secretly to get a shot of this strange man who took his mistress travelling with such an entourage.

When we arrived at New York the port's tugboats were on strike, and many ships waited in the roads (the equivalent of a marine parking-bay just outside a port). Waiting about for striking tugboat crews was not the kind of activity that the captain of *The Queen Elizabeth* engaged in. He docked his vast liner without their help in spite of the tides. His ship dwarfed the buildings on the wharf – and that was the first time I saw the skyline of New York. I have visited that city often since then and watched tall buildings fill out that skyline. Always it seems to get better. Now for the first time in my memory no cranes hang over the city and traffic is not disrupted by building works.

I couldn't make it here, so I'm going back to Didcot.

As I wandered down Madison Avenue I visited the great Atriums of New York's towers: the IBM building with its 30-foot high bamboos and Basement Art Gallery; what was once the AT & T [America Telecom & Telegraph] office – and called the Chippendale Building because of its similarity to a giant grandfather clock – is now the Sony Building. Undergoing conversion at ground level, it will become a shrine to Sony goods and the gods of electronics. Two small traders who rent space in the building still hold out against these changes; building work goes on around them. At 380 Madison Avenue is what I suppose will be the last of these remarkable buildings, this one with a foyer designed by Alberto Pinto, famous for his work on hotels.

Other buildings have not changed since I first set foot in New York: the brownstone church on Madison and the streets that radiate off it with their brownstone houses – still largely residential, they stay the same. Then there are the apartment blocks of Fifth Avenue opposite Central Park; if they have changed you would be hard pressed to know it. They are still the grandest apartments anywhere, looking out over the park side by side with the Pier and Sherry Netherland hotels. Across the square where the horsedrawn carriages wait is the Plaza Hotel. Nearby is the 21 Club where I ate on my first visit, and I still eat there. These are all names that New Yorkers have known for generations.

On 57th Street a block or two away is the new Four Seasons Hotel designed by I M Pei. Mussolini would have been proud of him – the public rooms are vast; marble and stone are used everywhere and the furniture has the shape and colour of the 1930s. It is less busy than Milan's Central Station and without a fascist iconography, but it has much the same feel about it.

Those who travel to New York must wonder why America chose Washington as its capital. The answer is simple – it comes to you as you walk in New York's streeks, drink in its bars, and eat in its restaurants. New York is not typical of America: New York is currently the capital of the world.

DEM BONES, DEM BONES. . .

THE American Museum of Natural History in New York is a formidable building. It looks the way a great museum should look, with large portico and flights of steps to its doorway. In front of it stands a statue of President Teddy Roosevelt on his horse. Roosevelt did not found the museum – that role was filled by Albert S. Bickmore; nor for that matter did he lay the museum's foundation stone; that function was carried out by another president, Ulysses S. Grant. No, Teddy Roosevelt was one of that strange breed of men who like to kill animals yet are intensely interested in their preservation, and he played an important part in the museum's history – indeed, a vital part. For when it opened in 1877 there was very little public interest and few people turned up for the ceremony, and by 1880 the museum set up to conserve the display animals long since extinct was on the verge of extinction itself. It was Teddy Roosevelt who saved the day: he acquired from the public purse a large sum of money to help them out. This is why he sits cast in bronze astride his horse on the steps. Somewhat of an embarrassment in this age of political correctness, but his presence cannot be escaped, whether it is in the hall named after him, with its cavorting skeletons of dinosaurs, some of them 50 feet high, or as you walk amongst the stuffed elephants, past the windows behind which herds of stuffed oryx graze.

If you spend a day or even a week in this museum looking at the animals and the remarkable collection of artefacts, you will see but a fraction of what has been collected since the Roosevelt days: two million moths and butterflies, 8.5 million invertebrates, and more dinosaurs, birds, spiders, animals, fossils and whole skeletons than any other museum in the world. Over three million artefacts and specimens, and among all these the skeleton of Barnum and Bailey's famous elephant, Jumbo; all these looked after by 200 scientists and their attendant technicians, porters and workmen, guides, office staff and public relations officers. All housed in a building of 1.2 million square feet – and all the time new specimens pour in. The fish department alone has 120 barrels of fish waiting to be catalogued and taken into the collection. The scale of the whole operation is remarkable: five whole storeys of dinosaurs bones – they call it the 'bone store', rack upon rack of pieces of dinosaur. Dinosaur eggs not by the dozen but by the gross.

The history of the museum is stuffed with characters. Barnum Brown – or Mr Bones as he was called – dug up more dinosaurs than any other man who ever lived. At Hell Creek he found the huge carnivorous dinosaur, Tyrannosaurus Rex; not one of those gentle grass-eating animals that we read about, with small heads and big bodies, so stupid that they ate themselves to extinction. Mr Bone's dinosaur was a beast whose bite was poisonous – because of the rotting flesh left between its teeth. In the 1930s he discovered at Howe Ranch near the base of the Bighorn Mountains a dinosaurs' graveyard, and sent 4,000 bones back to the museum in 144 cases weighing 35 tons. Then there was Roy Chapman Andrews. He started work at the museum scrubbing floors in the taxidermy department; fifteen years later, in 1922, he headed an expedition to the Gobi desert looking for the missing link. He did not find it, but he did find the only Baluchitherium skull ever found. So rare was this skull that Andrews hired bandits to transport it around China – then it was shipped back to America. Roy Chapman Andrews was the model for Indiana Jones.

Among all these wonders, I found the flies – two and a half million of them, case upon case, some so small they cannot be seen with the naked eye. I asked the curator which was his favourite, and without a moment's hesitation he replied, 'the New Guinea Antler fly, though I must say I am torn between the stagshorn and the elkhorn as to which variety I prefer'.

All that calcium

Appreciating Antiques

I WAS in New York. My visit coincided with the opening of the winter antique show at the Armoury on Park Avenue, and it was an event filled with tension: would the Crash of '87 take its toll on the Sales of '88? In the event, business boomed, partly because of the effect of the devalued dollar. Dealers in American antiques were selling their stock like the proverbial hot cakes. (This expression has always interested me, for if hot cakes did not sell they would soon become cold cakes, which I have always found perfectly edible.) Most of the American country furniture at the show sold within the first three days. The market seemed to be firm, and the dealers smiled.

Which object in the galaxy would I have bought if I was there to invest? Not the American furniture, for a start. To buy the art objects of a nation is to invest in the currency of that nation. There are easier ways of doing this, and easier places to do it than the winter antiques show. Therefore, I looked for objects with an edge – things that would appreciate disproportionately to the market. I came to the conclusion that these lay not in the various categories of antiques, like furniture or paintings, but in the price range of £15,000 to £25,000. There are fields – like Impressionist painting – where £25,000 will barely buy you a signature, let alone a painting. We must look elsewhere. China, for instance: £25,000 will take you among the best of European china. Glass: it will buy a stipple-enamelled glass by Wolfe or Greenwood, an unmarked glass by the Beilby family, even an important piece of 15th-century Venetian glass. Antiquities are a wide open field where values have lagged a long way behind the rise in prices in the art market.

Turner watercolours are still available at the upper end of my price bracket. Better prices of furniture, however, have risen well beyond this range; £100,000 is not an unusual price to pay for a Chippendale bookcase or even, believe it or not, for a single chair with its original needlework. There is still the possibility of buying furniture well, but only by concentrating on country pieces, or oak. Seventeenth-century needleworks fall nicely in my price bracket for the best among them. In short, this is what an aspiring collector must do: stay firmly with his chosen field, and buy the best and only the best. The best will have not only quality but will carry a fine provenance as well.

If you have investment in mind, always try to buy the best in its field. That is where the potential for appreciation lies, but always apply the two cardinal rules of collecting: can you afford it, and do you really want it? Next, remember that collecting is a lottery, not unlike the stock markets of the world, and the charm and hazard of it lies first in appreciating the rules, and then discovering exceptions to them.

These thoughts passed through my mind in New York when I was lunching at the 21 Club. This was founded during the Depression and is a club only in name. It is not the sort of club you will find in St James's Street. But it is a club in the sense that the faces of the staff and the customers never seem to change from visit to visit.

Some years back the 21 Club was taken over by Mr Swid and Mr Cogan – names that became etched on the London scene when they tried to buy Sotheby's. You will remember that they tried to defeat the Bond Street opposition to them which asserted that because they come from New Jersey they would alter everything by promising that they would alter nothing. In my view, among the half dozen most useless things in the world is a promise from a man

I discovered a neglected area — FRYING-PAN handles.

who desires to take over a business that he will not alter a thing. I never believe him. I do not believe that human beings are capable of leaving things alone. However, I have to report that the 21 Club is the exception to the rule. It is cleaner and tidier, but for all the world unchanged, and as I sat at my usual table drinking a fine white Burgundy, I recalled the unhappy days of the Sotheby's takeover bid when Mr Swid and Mr Cogan's promise was not believed, and Mr Taubman, a property developer from Detroit, was allowed to take it over instead.

He did not leave Sotheby's alone, and by doing what Mr Swid and Mr Cogan promised not to do, Mr Taubman restored its fortunes. The most constructive of these changes was the appointment of the Earl of Gowrie as chairman. For Mr Swid and Mr Cogan, by leaving the 21 Club alone, and Mr Taubman, by changing Sotheby's, it had all turned out for the best: the rule had operated and an exception had been demonstrated. Indeed, the only twinge of sadness I felt at this point was that the Earl of Gowrie was not there to share my Montrachet Marquis Laquiche 1978. He is the most congenial luncheon companion.

CHILD'S PLAY AND ADULT AVIDITY

THE cavernous city seems to be designed for the wind which it lets in at one end and out the other. The streets are flayed by it. New York is dirty and still the most competitive place in the world; with a charm that comes from its own violent attempts to be charmless. Shimmering new buildings, the latest of which have carefully considered roofs with shapes tending towards exotic that are only really visible from the river or from the upper storeys of their neighbours. These high polished containers are sited among dull brownstone houses so that boredom and tedium wrestle for first place. Pedestrians are everywhere, pushing past the pretzel sellers and beggars. The king of beggars is the man who sits in front of a church in Madison Avenue wearing several sleeping bags. He breaks away from his breakfast of Rice Crispies and seasonal fruit to suggest to passers-by that they give him $100. To judge by his ample proportions, the tactic has not been without some success.

It is a city overflowing with antiques and restaurants imported from all parts of the world, and, of course, it is filled with great collectors, and greater museums.

However, there is one family whose collection is not the greatest and whose museum is not the biggest, but both are by far the most interesting. This is the Forbes family of *Forbes* magazine (the 'capitalist tool') and they have their own gallery. It is a masterpiece. The driving force is Malcolm S. Forbes, assisted by his four sons, and their collections range from Fabergé to vintage films. The collection is magic and would be the high spot in the collection of a collector of collections.

The gallery is very small and you are drawn through it rapidly from childhood, through obscurity to old age, with glimpses of virtue and greed on the way. At the beginning are armadas of toy boats (accompanied by nautical music), then armies of toy soldiers (accompanied by military music). By pressing your eye to a round window you can see into a small boy's bedroom, or rather, what a big boy believes a small boy's bedroom ought to be. After childhood, the greed of adult life; enough Fabergé eggs to make at least a dozen omelettes.

The Forbes collection is too large for the gallery, so the exhibits are rotated from time to time and when I went there was Virtue Rewarded: romantic paintings. For example, a large canvas, 3 feet by 6 feet, painted by Richard Ansdell in 1861. It is titled *Hunted Slaves*, and depicts a coloured man and woman chopping up a pack of savage dogs with an axe. The catalogue entry states: 'Ansdell was well known for his depictions of sporting scenes and the hunt.'

Another jolly painting is Jerry Barrett's canvas showing Florence Nightingale receiving the wounded in Scutari in 1856, but then Victorian paintings of the British school are a bit like that; more lively in their technique than in their subject-matter. The French, on the other hand, were tackling apples and nudes, sunflowers and lily ponds.

Perhaps the most interesting part of the collection is a room full of trophies that commemorate every conceivable occasion. As a sometime collector of chickens, one I noticed was a shield inscribed 'Best Pen of White Leghorns, 1929–30 for Northamptonshire egg layers'. A more up-market trophy is the miniature silver palace given to King George V and Queen Mary by the residents of the North-West Frontier Province to mark a visit they paid to Peshawar.

The urn which once held the ashes of a Mrs Steward is in doubtful taste, but this collection has a taste all of its own, ranging from silver-mounted croquet balls to inscribed ashtrays. There are more than 200 trophies marking minor triumphs in minor lives, and their presence in this collection gives them a chance of near immortality. Then, to a fascinating collection of papers relating to the presidents of the United States. It is a fitting finale to the collection (if finale is the right word to use about a collection that grows and grows).

This collection is one I find captivating in the originality of its context and display. Outside, the streets are still cold, and I go straight to Grand Central Station, to eat – where else? Down to tiled arches created by the Gustavino family in the early 1900s that house the Oyster Bar.

For the collector of oysters, what a place. Oysters with names like Long Island Blue Point, Fanny Bay, Hog Island, Shookum, Kumonots and Nalpeques. Then there are several dozen varieties of fresh fish. The best seafood dishes that America has to offer are on the menu, and you can wash down your meal with a Bloody Mary, followed by a choice wine from California – there are more than 70 sorts.

A friend of mine lunching there was served by a waiter of rather more than ample proportions who rationalized his predicament thus: 'If you think I am going to starve myself to death to save my life, you're wrong.' I have mentioned this because there is a strange truth in this story – the same kind of truth that one finds so often in life. While the logic is perfect, the conclusion is flawed.

DEATH OF A SALESMAN

AT the close business on Friday the 13th – of October – Wall Street appeared to be in free fall. Investors had the weekend to think about this; and on the following Monday the London stock market opened well down. That same day, Christie's was having a sale of glass; 17th-,18th- and 19th-century items English and continental. It was not an important sale, most of the pieces were the kind that glass dealers would buy for stock; yet prices rocketed, sometimes reaching three times the estimate. I am an enthusiast for glass of all types, and I believe it has been grossly undervalued. Nevertheless, the prices at this sale left me wondering.

I was in New York at the time, and New Yorkers shrugged off the fall in the market – rather than worry about a crash that did not happen, they concerned themselves with an earthquake that did, in San Francisco. But New Yorkers are used to things changing quickly. Fashions change like the weather, and that week Monday and Tuesday were hot and sticky, while from Wednesday onwards the metropolis was wet and decidedly cold.

In painting, the fashions fly by: it is a full-time occupation in New York just to keep up with the trends in contemporary art. The city has also become the home of the blockbuster exhibition, such as the great one-man shows of Degas and Gauguin; there was also the Cubist Show, of Picasso and Braque, at the Museum of Modern Art. The prestige that we give to the leading artists of the 19th and 20th centuries allows these tremendous gatherings of their paintings to be assembled to tour the world.

There was a marked contrast between the Picasso-Braque exhibition, with several hundred paintings, and a Velazquez show with only 40 at the Metropolitan Museum (the best being the portrait of his servant, a painting which is on permanent exhibition in the museum anyway). The danger of damage caused to old masters by temperature change and in transit is so great that there will never be one-man shows of Piero della Francesca or Uccello; and the few known Giorgiones will not be seen in one place. I suppose, as time goes on, the larger shows will become the province of the lesser painters.

But the more fashions change, the more some things in New York – the shops on Madison Avenue, the Frick Collection, lunch in the 21 Club – seem the same, although everything is a little cleaner and tidier. One welcome change has come at the zoo, in Central park. It has been rejuvenated: the number of animals has been reduced, their habitats rebuilt, and a new emphasis placed on conservation and educational displays. The zoo used to be a source of embarrassment; now it is a place of beauty.

I have often had the feeling that magazine editors for whom I have worked over the years do not always believe the stories that I tell of the art and antiques trade. Say I were to suggest that in a town in the west of England there live an antiques dealer who bought four pieces for every one he sold and who would sell only to people he liked the look of – which was a small minority of those who came into his shop; say I were to go on to tell how the accumulation of stock drove his living quarters higher and higher up the terrace house that was also his premises; say I were to describe a dealer so obsessed with collecting and so indiscriminate in what he collected that he lived surrounded by his stock, the rooms heaped with antiques, so that only small burrows were left to move around in; say I were to claim that one day his obsession collapsed and crushed him. Would anyone be expected to believe me? A man killed by his own collection? Maybe, maybe not.

The story I tell is of the late R. F. Summerfield, a man gripped by the desire to accumulate. I cannot be absolutely certain that his collection played an active part in his death but it is a matter of fact that his body had to be winched from an upstairs window, there being no more convenient way out of the house.

The collection was sold by Christie's during most of one week at the end of one October. It was a sale extraordinary for its quantity – the catalogue came in three volumes, and offered a variety of goods probably greater than on any previous occasion – and exceptional for its lack of quality.

Why do people collect? And why do they collect items such as those in the Summerfield sale? What is the strange desire that drives humans in all cultures to sanctify places and objects, to collect all manner of things? I am still wondering.

LA Day-dreamer

I WAS in a no hurry to visit Los Angeles for the first time. I had heard only evil reports of the place: the smog; the riots; the traffic; the people – well, the ubiquitous 'they' told me that the people were truly awful. They don't drink, don't smoke and even disapprove of those who wear perfume. They barely eat (just lettuce and carrots), are obsessed with exercise (they jog all the time) and worst of all they go to bed early. How different I found the place. To me it was all a little like the South of France except the traffic is handled better. I love the weather; I love looking at the people, I love the place. And I keep going back and back.

On my last visit I set out to construct the perfect day. The best days begin with breakfast – and I don't mean coffee and a croissant in a hotel room. In downtown LA there is a place that understands what it should be like: The Pantry. They serve breakfast 24 hours a day, seven days a week – and so they should. The Pantry stands preserved among giant glass towers – a relic of the 1930s, its swing doors with flywire, its brown interior with Formica tables and green linoleum. The waiters show no hesitation – a brief good morning and a brief pause for your order. My waiter ordered for me – my dithering could have wasted his time. Eggs scrambled, two or four? Two say I. Bacon crispy, hash brown potatoes? I nodded. Hot cakes – a stack? Well, why not – in any case he was no longer there to argue with. Coffee? a voice asked, and my cup was filled. The Pantry is situated somewhere between the police department and the Town Hall. Tourists don't go there. Why should they. The place is the haunt of off-duty policemen and artisans who eat their breakfast there. A remnant from the age of Rockwell – partronized by Norman Rockwell's people.

Half an hour from downtown LA is Watts country, famous for its riots when it should be famous for its towers. The towers are no corporate or civic undertaking, rather the work of Simon Rodien, known as Sam, and built on some open land. They are Gaudiesque structures built of broken crockery and other odds and ends, and seem at first the work of a demented magpie. Then, as I wandered amongst them I realized that these strange buildings are but a maquette for masterpiece – and the man who built them, who all thought to be mad, a genius. Sam took 33 years to complete this work, then he just walked away, leaving the authorities with the problem of what to do with the towers. Happily they decided to keep them – in an ideal world they would be rebuilt 300 feet high in the centre of a city.

For lunch, I went to Rodeo Drive, the choicest street in town – actually just off Rodeo Drive – to The Ivy. I sat in its garden and watched the passing cars. The other customers watched me. The Ivy's garden is as like an English cottage garden as one in Somerset. It has no ivy, but every other plant, from hollyhock to delphinium, and all in flower. A garden complete with hay fever. I sneezed and sneezed and the diners watched in sheer horror – germs everywhere. The true charm of LA lies in the fact that it is one of the world's most sophisticated cities, yet still totally provincial – its street treelined, its housing suburban, all as peaceful as can be. Yet the city has a remarkable record for violence – the place is an illusion.

Among America's other great illusions is the cowboy. Gene Autry, a singing cowboy, made a great deal of money out of this illusion, though his greatest hit was *Rudolf the Red Nosed Reindeer*. His collection of art and artefacts from the Wild (and Hollywood) West is in the Gene Autry Heritage Museum. Since a child I have loved Westerns – what bliss, I would spend my afternoon there among Annie Oakley's gilded pistol, the Lone Ranger's spurs, not to mention his mask and red scarf, the guns and pistols of Teddy Roosevelt, and the official Colt firearms colletion. To spend time in this museum and to wander among the stuff of fact and fiction is to begin to understand America.

Where to dine? Well first I repaired to the bar of the Peninsular Hotel for a dry Martini. 'Straight up?' asked the bartender. He is a man who understands Martinis. I asked him where I should go to eat.

'A new place, Ciao Bella on Melrose.'

'Wonderful, can I use your telephone to make a reservation?'

'I am sorry sir, but we lost the telephone at lunchtime – a man made off with it,' he said, pointing at the empty portable phone stand.

Ciao Bella is an Italian resturant – pizzas and fun. The chef, from Milan, cooks Italian food the way Americans like it, and the Italian proprietor Mario Cesario is from just across Melrose Avenue where he runs Formula Uno, a second-hand clothing store of considerable distinction. The food is good, the customers beautiful, and Mario a generous and entertaining host. 'I am worked off my feet, I cannot keep up,' he states – when a place is fashionable in LA it is really fashionable. He took from his pocket a bundle of visitors cards printed with the names and addresses of women, each one annotated in Mario's own hand. 'Look at this, and I have only been open three weeks. How can I make time to see all these girls?' Such are the problems that beset restaurateurs in Los Angeles.

LA LORE

LOS ANGELES is not a town – not a city – not really a district – it is a world of near total fantasy. The people who live here are like actors in a play as they walk the streets, sit in the restaurants, go about their work, seemingly conscious of an unseen audience who watch – or perhaps they just act for each other. The citizens of Los Angeles dress for their roles as well and take some care in their choice of clothes, whether they buy them in the expensive shops of Rodeo Drive (there is one boutique in that street where you have to make an appointment just to gain entrance) or in the second-hand stores of Melrose Avenue, where young people crowd on a Sunday – literally crowd – to search through racks of second-hand clothes. These have become so popular in Los Angeles that manufacturers are now reproducing them, for the supply of the truly second-hand comes nowhere near to meeting the demand.

Los Angeles is a place of extremes: the marina at Marina del Ray is the largest in the world – most of the boats in it seldom put to sea; the largest street, Figueroa Street, stretches 26 miles – everything in Los Angeles is done to excess. The health clubs are wall to wall, the pet-supply shops are as supermakets would be in any other town. Indeed, sixty million people in America own cats, and while there are no figures for the feline population of Los Angeles, you can be sure that it is far and away above the average. I found one large store that only sells light bulbs – I had no idea that there were so many different kinds. Another shop that I visited specialized

Los Angeles Cat
chewing gum.

in full-sized dinosaurs – skeletons, I hasten to add, for it would not have surprised me one little bit to find them advertised as pets in the local paper. The car is supreme in Los Angeles, and one Toyota dealer alone – he has the name of Longo – sells 19,000 of these cars in a year. Like most cities Los Angeles has its ethnic quarters: but while it is not unusual to find a Chinatown or even (in Los Angeles) a Tokyo Town, you will also find a Korean Town, a Little Saigon and even a Little India.

It is an extraordinary place and most extraordinary of all are not Charlie Chaplin's old studios on La Brea near Sunset, nor the great production companies' studios, nor the Chinese Theatre (which is really a cinema), nor Disneyland. No, by far the strangest place to visit in the whole of Los Angeles is the Getty Museum. This museum perched in a valley overlooking the sea at Malibu is, so I'm told, the exact replica of a Roman villa formerly at Herculaneum – the Villa de Papyri built in California. There is nothing particularly odd about this, except that this vastly expensive structure filled with culture is cheek by jowl with a mass of other villas built in the styles of the 20th century – built for the pleasure of people who wished to live near the seaside. You can, in reality, only visit the museum by car – there are a whole posse of security men who direct vehicles up and down the narrow drive. The first question they ask is whether you have booked your parking space – without such a booking, unless you are driven, you will be turned away. The garage is truly impressive, a great cavern underneath the whole undertaking. It is not the least bit Roman – pure functional 20th-century America. Up a fire stair and, blow me there you are back in Herculaneum. Then there is the bookshop and the rather tacky restaurant with its machines and plastic tables that fill a garden designed for Roman ladies to take their pleasure in. Up another fire stair, a different world again. You could be walking through the galleries of the Wallace Collection what with the Louis XVI furniture and even a Goya. It really is a place of the most remarkable constrasts – wow, even for California, this is pushing it a bit.

Then there are the antiques, including both wonderful sculpture and pieces that give ground for wondering whether they were worth the freight to get them there. All this is housed in a series of rooms of which even the larger ones are small, while the smaller ones are so small entrance is forbidden. Upstairs is French furniture and superb-quality china, and paintings that span the history of art – or at least span its easier periods. Outstanding among them is Van Gogh's *Blue Irises*. As a private collection, this place is wonderful, as a museum, presumptuous. Why for goodness sake do the directors of great museums the world over shudder at the very name of the Getty – if these boys keep at it for a hundred years there still will be no comparison with their collections. The guidebook, entitled *Masterpieces in the Getty Collection*, proudly announced that many of the best things in the collection have been acquired since Mr Getty's death. There is no feeling among the pieces that they were collected with an unerring eye for quality. Nor is there the quirkiness that makes a collector's accumulation so interesting. This museum has money to buy what it will, but what it needs it cannot buy – for Mr Getty is dead.

IF THE BOOT FITS

THE cowboy boot started in Texas as civilization came to that part of American and cars took over from horses. The boot remained, so Texans learnt to drive cars in high-heeled boots. But what was convenient in the stirrup proved awkward on the pedal of an automobile. As the state became richer the boots became fancier – go to Texas and when you are introduced they will only look at your hat and your boots: your social status will be judged by these two accoutrements. In time the cowboys moved to Hollywood – the ones with the guns and horses that is – and they of course took their boots with them.

Now in Los Angeles there is barely a street that does not boast a shop selling cowboy boots. These shops, unlike normal shoe shops, do not have a range of footwear – if you sell cowboy boots you only sell cowboy boots; for the retailer of these exotic items there is no question of wearing anything else. Ready-made boots cost from $500, hand-made from $1,500, and full alligator boots from $8,000 – inconvenient things to own, alligator boots, for if you travel you will spend a good deal of your time explaining to customs officers just why you are wearing a large chunk of CITES-listed reptile (CITES is the convention for international trading in endangered species). You can argue that you did not kill it, you can argue that it has been dead for a hundred years – it will do no more than prolong the discussion when you have just got off a long flight. Avoid boots made of endangered species like the plague. So when offered exotic boots by a salesman, say no, ask for fancy instead. The range is extraordinary – from boots with oil-drilling rigs up their sides (your own if you have oil wells, someone else's if you don't) to cactus and barbed-wire designs. These boots are likely to be made of calf skin inlaid with kangaroo hide. If you want fancy toes, ostrich is the hide to choose – your boots will then have small pimples all over them. Ostrich skin does not, however, come cheaply – a pair of breeding ostriches can cost £25,000.

It is obvious as you visit these shops and see the rows and rows of the boots, all in different colours, materials and styles that before long these remarkable objects will be collected. Indeed they are already being collected – there is a thriving market in second-hand boots. Aficionados of the Western boot will tell you that it is a great mistake to buy a new pair, far better to get a pair that has already been worn in: 15 per cent of hand-made boots are returned to the makers with the words, 'these do not fit'. The makers will tell you that this is because the people who return them are unused to wearing cowboy boots, which are made for riding not walking. Be that as it may, a good second hand pair is probably a better bet anyway: these boots are made to outlast people, and you can sometimes go through a dozen new soles with little sign of wear to the boot itself. The problem of course is that second-hand boots fetch higher prices than brand new ones – even if they have been custom-made to fit you.

One smart pair I came across was made of cream leather inlaid with rhinestones. The salesman told me that they had been used in the movies in the 1950s; he was unsure by whom, but a star no less. I could have them for $5,000 dollars.

'But they don't fit me.' (I have the oddest feet, nearly as wide as they are long.)

'I thought that you were a collector.'

'So I am.'

'Well these are a collector's item.'

'Well who did they belong to?' By way of answer he reduced the price to $3,500.

A remakable pair called The El Rey The III boots took three months to make. Of black alligator (not for travellers) inlaid with 24 carat gold encrusted with 384 diamonds and rubies, they were made in 1951 and cost $5,000. They have twice been stolen and are now said to be worth $30,000. When exhibited they come with their own armed guard. These boots are, I suppose, the top end of the range. But you can still put together, without, it seems, too much trouble, a remarkable collection of boots carrying the symbols of the States, other people's favourite horses, swooping eagles, or just plain with initials. For that matter you can pass idle hours tramping round the boot stores of LA looking for a pair of boots that, soft with use, fit your feet exactly and, like I did, find only that your feet get so sore you can barely walk on them. I went back to my hotel for a long bath. However, the next day, inspired by Tyler Beard's great book *The Cowboy Boot* and his words 'cowboy boots give you an attitude – they can be euphoric', I was out again searching for those boots that will perfectly fit my feet. I am afraid I still am.

THE GREAT ESCAPISM

DURING the last year it has been almost impossible to pick up a newspaper and find good news in it, while to switch on the television or the wireless is to be told only tales of gloom, whether the subject is the monarchy, the church, or the state of our nation. Shops seem almost perpetually in a state of sale time; the tourists keep a tight grip on their purses; the auction rooms announce triumphs, but they have a hollow ring to them; antique dealers fail – even the great dress houses are feeling the pinch. How on earth can one get away from it all? Well, I hit upon the solution while visiting Los Angeles, a city where reality has very largely become make-believe. I spent the day at Universal Studios – a place where reality has never existed, where make-believe is more believable than any reality you may come across, and I may say that there is very little to be depressed about there, where they made the runaway bestseller *Jurassic Park*.

I set out after a hearty breakfast – for those who have never visited the worlds of make-believe that emanate from California, take my tip and eat beforehand lest hunger persuades you to indulge in a bite to eat while there; the results of such a meal are terribly real. I arrived at 7.30 a.m., and already the park (which had opened at 7 a.m.) was busy. I followed the crowd through the theme park, which is as good or bad as most theme parks, and I suppose if you are interested in how to perform a gunfight on the hour every hour, to fall from a rooftop apparently shot (covered in red paint), then you will enjoy this place. Conan the Destroyer calls up dragons to slay; the characters from *Miami Vice* go through a nerve-chilling routine of their most exciting stunts; *Star Trek* is a masterpiece of modern technology only bettered by *Back To The Future* 'the ride' – its advertisement warns you to 'prepare to scream through the future', and in part it is right; almost everyone who goes on this ride screams most of the time.

There is little escapism in this park, however, with its heaving and squealing mass of humanity. Move quickly on and descend by the giant escalator down several hundred feet (an experience that makes the best that London Transport and their Underground system have to offer seem tame by comparison) to Universal's actual studios, to a world of magic that has given us *The Hunchback of Notre Dame* – and Paris is still there; *Spartacus* – Rome is still there; *The Sting* – New York is still there. Board a tram and tour this world where the unbelievable happens and leaves you untouched to head for the next event. The tour of Universal's back lot is really something; it has, apart from everything else, the most incredible collection of buildings, a textbook of 19th-century architectural styles beautifully built in wood, chickenwire and plaster – accurate in every detail. The guide, a personable young lady with a considerable sense of humour, announced that we were travelling up New York Street – and indeed, it looked for all the world just like parts of New York where the 19th century has survived. She added, 'Actually it can become a street in any of the world's cities'. I was about to ask how but she anticipated me. 'We change the signs, the colours and a few of shapes – the street however stays the same, it just *seems* different.'

This is a world where many strange events *seem* to happen. We approached a bridge – it started collapsing before my eyes. We just made it across in time to look over a shoulder and watch it reassemble itself. 'We filmed Superwoman jumping up on to that bridge – actually we filmed her jumping down and played the film backwards,' said our guide. We were all amazed. She went on: 'It did not work' – we were totally amazed. 'Superwoman's hair flew up as she jumped down – when we played it backwards it seems as if she was being pulled up on to the bridge by her hair.' I would have loved to have asked, 'What on earth did you do?' but I am afraid I had not the slightest chance; the lady carried on. 'We shot it again – we put a hat on her.'

We survived the collapsing bridge only to be caught in a flash flood and pursued by King Kong – a giant gorilla 25-feet high who killed a helicopter just for us. (The animal used in the original film was only a few inches high.) Jaws attacked our train; Moses – or perhaps an assistant, for it was a bank holiday – parted the Red Sea so that we could cross safely to *Gilligan's Island* – despite mines that had been left behind from some maritime drama of the Pacific. They exploded but we passed unharmed. We then became involved in an avalanche, and the *pièce de résistance* was our adventure when we just happened to be passing though a Manhattan subway station in the middle of an earthquake. We were narrowly missed as a train crashed into a bus that had fallen through from the street above severing the water main. I am happy to report that we also escaped the flood and avoided electrocution by current from loose powercables. All this only to be nearly frightened to death by the House on the Hill from *Psycho*. All in all it was a jolly eventful ride despite nobody setting fire to Atlanta, and by and large it made the tragedies that the media search high and low for each day seem quite tame.

EIGHT

INTERNATIONAL AFFAIRS

THE WEALTH OF NATIONS

COLLECTORS with great wealth are different from the rest of us. For most collectors, habits vary from nation to nation, but for those who inhabit the stratosphere, there is an international taste that varies only from time to time. It makes no difference whether the seriously rich live in Tokyo or Paris or London or New York, they collect the same objects; French impressionists and French furniture always, although these have now been joined by works from modern European artists and, in some cases, the abstract expressionists.

All are symbols of wealth, and the wealthy fight for them. Witness, for example, the battles over the last three paintings by Vincent Van Gogh to appear in the saleroom. They were purchased by mystery buyers for prices that appear truly remarkable considering the provenance of many of those paintings.

It is only six decades ago that the elder Gimpel – whose son, Gimpel fils, founded the gallery in London – left Holland with a bundle of Van Gogh's paintings. At the customs, he was stopped and asked what they were. 'My own work,' he replied. 'I am taking them to Paris to see if I can sell them.'

'I think you will need good luck,' replied the customs inspector, who, at the time, perfectly reflected the buying public's view of the works of Van Gogh.

Since then, France has adopted that artist, along with Picasso, Dali, Giacometti and a host of other painters and sculptors. France promoted them and, in the fullness of time, this chauvinistic approach to collecting was varied to include them as honorary Frenchmen when the volume of interested money increased at a rather greater rate than the availability of masterpieces by desirable dead artists.

The number of evenings at Sotheby's and Christie's when the fantastic is sold for millions to the mysterious in front of a dinner-jacketed, champagne-mellowed audience increases to the point of boredom. For their part, the commentators and critics hunger for failure, anticipating the Van Gogh sale that fails to attract a bid in the room. I'm afraid that if these people wait for this they will starve. The super rich are always with us.

The rest of us will go on buying what we like, and that is usually a reflection of where we come from. Each nation tends to buy its own art – the French buy French, Germans buy German. The Canadians and Australians seldom buy anything other than work by native artists; the Americans have a very strong market in American art.

The French, who invented the word chauvinist, practise its meaning in the extreme. Let us take the case of a shrewd French collector on whose walls hung works by Monet, Manet and Renoir. In his gallery he had a large and magnificent Turner on an easel.

Could you remove the 'Turner' signature —

No problem

RESTORER GRADE I

— and replace it with 'Monet'?

His guests would declare it a great work and ask who painted it. The collector would reply that it was attributed to an English painter named Turner, but added that it must be a fake, because no English artists painted that well.

I was in Australia recently and enjoying its orgy of self-indulgence. Hardly a week goes by without a sale of Austrlaian paintings, furniture and pottery. There is also bric-à-brac, which is described as Australian and includes anything with an Australian trademark stamped on it. The enthusiasm for anything Australian seems almost boundless. Of course, this was exaggerated by the bicentenary, a great Australian party with parades of tall ships and Aboriginals who came to protest, but, like many of the rest of us, enjoy a good party too.

The celebration was accompanied by significant cultural events devoted to Australia's history: her way of life; her marine biology; her ships; her trains; and, indeed, a warehouse devoted entirely to her bric-à-brac. The bicentenary made the multinational inhabitants of this country supremely aware that they are Australians, and of their land and its art.

To an amateur collector, all this might appear as a glut on the market. But the real collector knows this is not the high point of a market, but the beginning of a better one. Opportunities like these occur once every 200 years or so.

The line between rarity and obscurity is very narrow. In time the great works by Australian painters such as Sir Sidney Nolan, Arthur Boyd and Russell Drysdale will rise in price along with the best pottery. (The price of bric-à-brac rises and falls with position.)

There is a lesson here for the discerning collector: spot an emerging nation – and there will be plenty in the next two centuries – and buy the product of its people. As the country becomes rich, so will its people. As they become rich, they will collect the work of their forebears; the shrewd collector will already have discovered the value of these trappings.

A Mugs Game?

Collectors are quite as strange as the objects they collect, and no less rare. An ordinary collector is a man with 27 mugs commemorating various anniversaries of the royal family, who is delighted to discover another example in Padstow during his holidays. A true collector will not be satisfied until he has 700 commemorative mugs, covering every table and mantle-shelf in a house in which the windows do not open because there are regiments of royal mugs on the sills. His toothbrush stands in a mug; he drinks his tea from a duplicated or chipped mug; there are flowers in the mug beside his bedside table, and there are more mugs in unpacked boxes in the hall. Indeed, the unlucky collector is the man who does not own a warehouse and has to pay the admirable firm of Pitt and Scott to store his treasures.

I have known collectors who purchase a masterpiece but don't bother to unwrap it when it arrives. (Perhaps they collect parcels.) Unlike casual buyers, collectors do not visit shops, they haunt them. For them, collecting is an occupation – a crusade almost. The rest are furnishers and decorators.

True collectors are legendary figures, like the man who collected spongeware jugs and mugs. One warm Sunday evening he visited a pub in Hampshire; above the bar was hanging a set of spongeware mugs, originals embossed with the name of the pub. These simple half pint and quart drinking vessels were standard in country pubs in the late 18th century.

While he tried to buy the set, our collector was made to spend much time lifting trees. Eventually, he made an offer for the whole pub, but, life being what it is, the pub was sold to a man who collected pubs.

A true collector of chickens – and I was once one myself – is not interested in birds of the sort that end up trussed in Sainsbury's, but in breeds like the Transylvanian Naked Neck and Light Brahmas. I had 75 varieties myself, and since the names are more exotic than the birds, it just shows that true collectors will collect almost anything.

Some collectors are men who become famous first and collectors latter, like Pierpont Morgan, who collected Renaissance paintings in much the same way lesser breeds collect royal commemorative mugs. However, the Pierpont Morgan tale that endears him to me concerns nothing grander than a pearl tie pin – a functional as well as decorative object in those days. The jeweller was instructed to buy it and send it to Morgan's house. He did so, enclosing a bill for $5,000.

The jeweller was surprised, naturally, when the tie pin was returned to him in its box. Morgan also sent a cheque, for $4,000, and a note saying: 'I like the tie pin, but not the price. If you agree to $4,000, cash the cheque and return the tie pin to me.' The jeweller was incensed. Since he believed he had always dealt honestly with Morgan, this cast doubt on all their dealings. If he had said $5,000, that was his price. So he took the cheque and tore it in half. Some time later he was putting the pin back into stock and he idly opened its box. Inside, there was no tie pin. Only a cheque for $5,000, signed Pierpont Morgan.

Morgan had been playing a game, for he knew that the jeweller was an honest man, for even rich collectors cannot afford to buy from dishonest men. For myself, I do not care too much whom I sell to, but I am very selective about whom I buy from.

In the end, when you buy antiques – or anything else of consequence – no matter how hard you look and check, you rely on the person who sells it to you. Integrity is not a matter of will. It is either part of man's soul or it is not. The word honest has this in common with the words unique and pregnant: you cannot be a little bit of any of them.

THE PRICE OF TRANSGRESSION

HERE are three stories about the dreadful effect on talented people of three great human failings: pride, greed, and jealousy. They are sad stories because each of these failings destroys – slowly, but with absolute certainty – its victim.

First, pride. There were two Bond Street antiques dealers of great repute. Their shops were opposite each other and they were adversaries. Their rivalry took the form of uttering mildly deprecating remarks about the other's stock ('too brightly painted', or 'too highly gilded', one would say of a piece in the other's window display) and each was so proud of his own stock that he could not bring himself even to look at the furniture across the road.

One of these dealers acquired a bow-fronted commode of such beauty and quality that it might have been made by Chippendale himself. This commode stood in the back of the shop and eventually attracted the attention of a discriminating Knightsbridge dealer, who bought it. By a remarkable coincidence, just as it was being delivered to his shop he received a visit from the other grand Bond Street dealer.

'What a piece,' exclaimed the latter when he saw the commode. 'What's the price?'

The Knightsbridge dealer contented himself with adding a modest profit to his purchase price (he doubled it). After all, he had owned the piece for only a few hours.

'Where did you get it?' asked the Bond Street man.

'I'm afraid I cannot disclose where I acquired it,' replied the Knightsbridge man, a trifle pompously, 'but I can tell you that I'm frightfully pleased with it and if it is of no use to you just let me get it into the shop and with one telephone call I'll be able to sell it.'

At this the Bond Street man threw himself between the commode and the shop's front door. The removal man stood by, uncertain whether it was coming or going.

'It's mine,' he cried. 'Load it up again and deliver it to my Bond Street shop. At once.'

It is questionable whether he would have displayed the same enthusiasm had he known that this commode had sat for months in the back of the shop across the road at half the price. He did not know because his pride had not allowed him to look. So he paid.

Next, greed. There was a shop in Mayfair that dealt in arms and armour. It was a paradise for small boys, although I am bound to say that when I grew up, I lost none of my enthusiasm for that emporium.

One day the owner was away at a country sale and left an assistant in charge. Shortly after 3 p.m. a well-dressed man, obviously possessed of a few quid, entered the shop. The assistant did not know much about arms and armour, but he did know a rich drunk when he saw one. The customer began to enthuse about a pair of pistols, cocking them, firing them, pointing them at passers-by in the street. Making a proper nuisance of himself. As he did this the assistant noticed that the price tag had become detached. It read £750, and when the well-dressed man asked the price, the assistant told him £1,500. Done, was the reply, and having written a cheque on the spot, the gentleman left, taking the pistols with him.

On hearing this story when he returned to the shop, the owner – an honourable man – was not impressed by the assistant's enterprise. He telephoned the customer that same evening at his home and said that a terrible mistake had been made. The pistols were not really for sale, but since the fault was entirely his, he would be grateful if the customer would return the pistols and take a cheque for £3,000 for the inconvenience and embarrassment.

But greed, fed by the deep suspicion of the truly ignorant, had taken root. 'It is no good trying that one on me,' the customer said, 'if you have undersold them, that's your bad luck. A deal is a deal. Sorry.'

Puzzled, the dealer kept the money. More important, he retained his honour. The customer's greed was his own affair.

Finally, the worst of these failings, jealousy. This story took place in Melbourne, where a dealer had the good luck (some might call it skill) to turn up a cedar bureau bookcase of Australian manufacture and recognize it as possibly the earliest known piece of Australian furniture. It was quite fine, not a masterpiece, but its extreme rarity made it much sought after by Australians.

The find was a triumph, but it has been spoiled by the behaviour of a rival dealer in Sydney, specializing in Australiana. He spends a good deal of time debunking the man from Melbourne and his bureau bookcase. He does not offer any evidence. Indeed his suit comes down to this: if the bureau bookcase were any good it would be in his shop in Sydney. He is jealous, and it is destroying him, and the story contains a moral for dealers everywhere. It is better to spend time improving your own understanding than to waste time knocking the competition.

When a customer reveals that he has bought an object elsewhere and you know that it is half the quality and twice the price of one you have yourself, the best thing is to smile and say 'very nice – indeed wonderful – very good of its kind'. You should never – please, never – discourage a collector.

CAUTIONARY TALES

THERE is a need for these tales of caution, for the world of collecting is unsure and savage for the unwary. For that matter, it is a hairy place for the extremely wary. Know this: let all your collecting be for pleasure. Take pleasure in your success; and pleasure in your failures.

The make-up of a collector is a compound of many emotions: the desire to own; an admiration of beauty; the urge to complete a set or pattern; perhaps even to own a piece of some famous person, like collecting scraps of Picasso's work for the purpose of identifying with Picasso. (There is little merit in these poor offerings for their own sake.) This motive is the same as that of the native people in Hawaii who killed and intended to eat Captain Cook so as to acquire his great skill as a navigator.

Collecting can take the collector into another world, if only for a moment. With the help of the collection, a collector can be demonstrate to an admiring public his intellect, his taste, and his knowledge. He can boast without saying a word. He can bore an audience that is nonetheless capitivated by, say, his stamps. He can move up and down the social scale by following or rejecting fashion, if he collects on a grand enough scale.

The Saatchi brothers, Charles and Maurice, are a case in point. They are the contemporary equivalents of the Earl of Arundel, whose fine collection of marbles found its way to a patch of wasteland by the Oval after his death. The gasometer stands there now. The Earl's heirs, who had disposed of the marbles, received a writ from the old London County Council. Remove them or we'll sue, said the LCC, and all but a few of these great marbles became mortar used for building London.

What price, in 50 years or so, that fine museum the Saatchis built in St John's Wood? Will we always admire the work of modern Americans like Julian Schnabel? But these questions do not matter. It is the courage to collect that must be admired. Not the collection. Grand collecting can bring fame or failure, as with the greatest of all collectors, Charles I. His collection was destroyed and scattered across Europe by the rebels who also melted down King Alfred's crown to pay the army.

Collecting brings out all the instincts of the gambler. Not the gambler who, at the roulette wheel, knows in a moment whether he has won or lost. The collector will wait for years to have his judgement endorsed. Or to wallow in the admiration of his contemporaries. Or gently to massage his ego in the certain knowledge that he is right and the rest of the world wrong. The last characteristic of a collector is that he has a store where he keeps the objects of his admiration. Until he has a great quantity of these objects – more than he can ever use himself – he is no more than an interior decorator furnishing a residence.

My first cautionary tale is about the greatest motivating force among collectors. This is greed, whether justified by beauty, or by the desire to complete, or even by the collection of objects for which the collector has no need whatsoever. Greed comes in many forms, and is often carefully disguised. Recently, I became a victim of it myself. Over many years, I have consumed my fair share of claret. (To be honest, I have consumed the shares of a few of my friends, as well.) Burgundy, or, rather, red Burgundy, I have always shunned for no better or worse reason than the strange business of various houses each owning a few rows of vines in the same vineyard. It is not that I do not like the taste, just that I have never understood it. Claret – or, as the French call it, Bordeaux – is simple. Claret is my drink.

God, I hate Burgundy.

However, one July four years ago, led astray by a group of friends, a trip to Burgundy ws arranged. Vineyard after vineyard; neat lines of barrels; rows of glasses, elegant tapering glasses; heady, heavy lunches. The liquor was beautiful and rare, and I was overcome by a desire to be part of that rustic society, and to appear at home among these stout and florid men. I am a man who needs no Burgundy, but prices were tossed about, and a bargain struck. Not one but seven hogsheads were acquired. It was a set, perfect in its symmetry. It had the right amount of white wine, a quantity bottled in magnums, the right balance of heavy wine to lighter wine for afternoon drinking. The conversation itself was pure pleasure. It was a collector's piece. In ignorance and self-indulgence.

The years passed. My friends told me of the greatness of the vintage I had acquired. Its crop was destroyed. It had become an investment. It was a great investment. My folly had been turned to profit. Recently, I decided to realize my profit and I called the merchant whose company had been so beguiling. He told me that my wine was lost.

– Lost?

– But not lost beyond recall, he said.

– But lost?

– Not really lost, he said. Just not available.

– Why so?

– A company had been taken over. There was confusion.

– But what happened?

– The receivers, apparently.

– And the money I'd paid four years ago?

– Well, it always was a bit of a gamble, wasn't it, old boy?

I am the victim of this cautionary tale. The reason I bought the wine was greed. I did not want it and justified it by the allure of a profit. My motive should have been pleasure. I should have stuck to claret and drunk it with my friends. We would all have felt like princes, for fine French wine is one of the world's great excellences, but it is bought and sold by lesser men.

The Large and the Small of It

It is not necessary to be a collector to realize how small events can at times have much greater consequences. There is no need to look any farther than Sir John Pope-Hennessy, who, like some ghostly stoker from the age of steam, shoveled coal into the furnace of debate about the Victoria and Albert Museum. His outburst contained a number of points that ought not to go unquestioned.

For instance he criticized Elizabeth Esteve-Coll, the present director, for exhibiting the Elton John Collection. If he is right, the Ashmolean in Oxford must also be equally guilty for giving space to Tradescant's collection of souvenirs and contemporary junk. But it must be said that that exhibition has been a great success. It has run for centuries.

Sir John blamed the troubles at the V & A on Margaret Thatcher, then Prime Minister, with whom his relationship got off to a bad start when she was Minister of Education. She gave him a glass of sherry and asked him to suggest three china services in the museum from which she would select one to fill the display cabinets in her office. She chose the one he did not like. His bitterness began with that trifling incident.

Sir John's prejudices were exhibited once more when Margaret Thatcher took a tour conducted by himself and was interested only in the conservation department, especially when she was shown two ladies sticking fabric together with glue. He was even more surprised when she quoted the chemical formula for the glue. It was sad that he did not pay more attention; for it was discovered later that the glue used by the conservation department is bad for fabrics and in time turns them black.

The curiosity is that a junior cabinet minister should go from a lunchtime glass of sherry to become Prime Minister of Great Britain, and that Sir John Pope-Hennessy should become known as a vindictive and offensive old man rather than for the scholarship to which he devoted his life.

I have been collecting Venice again and took comfort from the incident in 1305 when the citizens attempted to displace Damonte Tiepolo, the doge, who was holed up in his palace. Led by a standard-bearer, the avenging citizens streamed towards the Bocca di Piazza, one of the arches leading into St Mark's Square. Above, a lady watching from a window was so enthusiastic that she dislodged a stone mortar from its sill. The mortar fell and hit the standard-bearer on the head. When he dropped to the ground, the standard fell with him, and the crowd ran. It was a small thing, but it saved the doge.

There is nothing small about the canvases of the fashionable contemporary Italians, Enzo Cucchi, Francesco Clemente and Sandro Chia, the escalating price of whose work illustrates another theory of mine: that if you propose to invest in art, choose work from artists working in a booming economy. I obtain greater pleasure from work produced on a more modest scale – the glass of Murano.

This is not the tacky glass to be seen in so many shops in Venice, which is not made in Murano at all, but imported from Tuscany, the former Yugoslavia or even Taiwan. The glass I refer to was made from the 1930s to the 1950s by Barovia e Tossa, or Venini glass by Flavio Poli, or Zecchin glass by Martinuzzi and Scarpa. It is a large subject that takes a little learning, but it is certainly worth the trouble.

Incidentally, they cook as well as make glass in Murano, and the local speciality is a dish of eels called *bisato sullara*. (Men working in the furnaces used to place a tray of eels, bay leaves, olive oil and white wine at the mouth of the furnace where it steamed till lunch time.)

In the 15th century, the Venetians had a small passion for collecting dwarfs, dead and alive, in glass, china and stone. The fashion began, it appears, near Vicenza in a Palladian villa. Legend has it that this villa, opposite the Villa Rotunda, was built to house the daughter of a noble family who was born a dwarf. Since they were concerned for her happiness, her parents decided that she must never know that she was so much smaller than her contemporaries. So, they built a high wall around the property and collected a team of dwarfs to live with her there. All her life, she believed she was normal, and when she died her fellow dwarfs were so sad that they turned to stone. These stone dwarfs can now be seen along the top of the wall of the Villa Valmorana.

Isabella D'Este, who possibly was the sitter for Leonardo's *Mona Lisa*, was another such collector, though she preferred live dwarfs. Quarters were designed especially for them in her palace in Mantova. In any event, she was a great collector. Once she tried to acquire a night picture from Giorgione, was told that none was available and that in any case he had just died.

The dealer recommended a Bellini instead. There was much haggling about the price and the number of figures to be included in the painting. A poet had to be employed to think up a narrative subject, and some of the fee paid to the dealer went missing. The painting was three years late.

That was in the 15th century; the art world does not change much in matters large or small.

BEAUTY AND THE BEASTS

LONDON'S Victoria & Albert Museum is one of the greatest collections in the world. It is a place where masterpieces beyond price are exhibited check by jowl with objects so mundane that you would pause before allowing them space in the attic. This phenomenal collection is presided over by Elizabeth Esteve-Coll, a name with something of a ring to it. If you believe Sir John Pope-Hennessy, one of her predecessors, a ring is all there is to it. She is 'ignorant of the principles of museology and of the history of this particular museum', Sir John wrote in a remarkable exhibition of contemptible manners.

Along with his allies in the art trade, Sir John maintains that until Esteve-Coll's decisive reorganization of the V & A, it was a place full of learning. Now, he tells us, this woman 'who enjoys the title of director' is endangering the collection. The reason is that she wants the people who stuff the museum with learning to spend more time entertaining the public – especially as they are now paying customers and the state will no longer finance our great museums in the style to which they are accustomed.

Sir John and his ilk suggest that the unfortunate Esteve-Coll is conspiring to undermine exalted standards of curatorship and learning. If he believes that, I would invite him to inspect the work of the department with responsibility for the welfare of the V & A's glass collection. The place is a shambles. Dirty, it displays little if any attempt to describe the origins and background of most of the exhibits, no matter whether the audience be made up of scholars or peasants. Compare this with the reserve collection at the Metropolitan Museum in New York, where the objects are clean and carefully displayed, and all the department's information is on the museum computer and easily retrieved by a helpful young man.

Pope-Hennessy has accused Esteve-Coll of ignorance, among many other things. Surely it is clear, even to the most untutored observers among us, as we walk through the V & A's glass collection, that something went badly wrong with a system that was stuffed with scholarship. The museum is not a university. It owes its debts to a much wider public than Sir John and his cronies.

Time spent in Paris is always pleasurable. To find a Gauguin exhibition at the Grand Palais was a bonus. The paintings, rich in their colours, seductive in their subjects, simply glowed. To stand in the small and overcrowded room where the Tahitian paintings were mostly hung was to be close to paradise. Gauguin's awkward figures and jigsaw-like colouring seemed so perfect in their very imperfection. In *The Two Tahitians*, of 1899, one of them holds a flower, the other a tray of red fruit in juxtaposition to her breast, an absorbing prelude to my lunch at the Plaza Athénée.

To see Gauguin, it is necessary to travel to Paris. To view one of the world's best, and possibly most famous, flower shows there is no need to travel any further than the Royal Hospital, Chelsea.

When the Chelsea Flower Show opens, serious collectors will ignore the displays of garden furniture and machinery around the edges. These stalls are for the mechanic *manqué*. The serious collector heads for the centre of the mêlée – the long alleys of flowers in the main tent. Stalls of wild flowers, of irises, of peonies, of new roses and old roses, vie for attention with stalls of mixed flowers, displays from the horticultural departments of our boroughs, fly-eating plants and cacti in a thousand varieties.

The star of the show is always the new rose named after some TV personality, but that is not what makes it a flower collector's paradise. In the grounds of the Royal Hospital you could collect only the catalogues and still come away with an impressive collection.

But if it is wild flowers that you dream of, go to Perth in Western Australia in September. There, in Kings Park, more than 2,000 acres of natural bush in the middle of the city, are 8,000 species of wild flower. On those cool September mornings their combined scent has a beauty I have never experienced elsewhere. Kangaroo paw, native iris, the banksia shrub – plants so exotic they have been collected for years and were growing in conservatories in Europe long before the state was settled.

In this peaceful and strange park there are also avenues of ghost gums, each with a plaque to commemorate a Western Australian soldier killed in the First World War. It is a moving experience just to read them: Hall, George F., 10th Australian Light Horse, killed in action, Palestine 19. 4. 17; Fred Thomas, killed, Pozières, France, 1916. These men died in a far-away continent more than 30 years before the centenary of their state. The white-tailed black cockatoos circle and shriek in the wind and under these trees the wild flowers grow in plumes not unlike the emu feathers that decorated the slouch hats these dead men wore.

The flowers are like a great posy on their memorial. Never is the idea of war more beautiful, never is the futility of war more certain, than when you stand in this small park in the most remote city in the world.

OLIVER FORD: A FAREWELL

OLIVER Ford, decorator to Her Majesty Queen Elizabeth, died on 17 October 1992. He died suddenly while standing in the Great Hall of his home at Lacock – in his later years he was hard to entice from there. Virtually retired from his business, he devoted his time to his garden, and a remarkable garden it is. His reluctance to travel may well have misled those who knew him only latterly, for he was in fact a great traveller, not by any means a tourist, but a real traveller who undertook long journeys. He was the most congenial of travelling companions as well, filled with humour, seldom grumbling although he in fact disliked foreign food, preferring steak and chips to curry and the other concoctions of the Orient. In Singapore, after four days of Chinese food – I am myself addicted to Chinese cooking – I asked him where he wished to dine. He chose a Japanese restaurant, one specializing in *tepanani*. I was a bit surprised at this, but he ordered only chopped steak and quietly bemoaned the missing chips.

One night we visited Bugis Street which was, before its re-development, a traffic-free streeet. Traffic-free in those days not by city ordinance but because the restaurateurs whose establishments were cheek by jowl along the street, having filled the pavement with chairs and tables, had started putting them where traffic might have been. The street was filled with tourists who in their turn became part of the spectacle that tourists came to watch. These were the days of the Vietnam War. This street was pure theatre. There were soldiers and sailors who, as the evening grew late, drank and sang; local musicans and vendors came as the audience, lubricated by Singapore beer, became generous with money. Then began the parade of the transvestites – soon they were all muddled up. Sailors, tourists and transvestites all on the most friendly of terms. Oliver Ford and I watched all this, we laughed and I suppose we may have sung. Then, unexpectedly, a transvestite sat on Oliver Ford's lap. 'I am a pretend Mary Poppins,' this exotic creature announced, though how he came to that conclusion eludes me, for a more far-fetched version of that demure creature Mary Poppins would be hard to find. Oliver Ford protested, the transvestite kissed him on his bald head and left for new pickings. The soldiers and sailors were all drunk, the tourists began to go home, the pimps became more insistent, fights broke out, bottles and glasses smashed. We headed for our hotel, and as we climbed from the trishaw Oliver Ford, offering to pay, found his wallet had gone. Pretend Mary Popins had not been quite as innocent as she wished us to believe.

Oliver Ford was direct about his life: 'camp as a row of tents' he often used to say, and to a female client who boasted of her dining-room chairs: 'My dear, I have more chance of being Queen Anne than those chairs'. But this was the stuff of London. I also knew him in the Australian outback where there is red dust and vehicles bogged down easily. Driving the 1,500 miles of the journey from Perth to Broome by the inland route through Meekatharra, Nullagine and Marble Bar, stopping in the near ghost town of Cue, with its wonderful Victorian buildings, the gold all gone and most of the people with it. The bandstand in the main street long without musicians. On that trip we were novices. My wife Romilly, Oliver and I, we nearly perished.

It is a strange fact about travelling in the north-west of Australia, a land of low scrub that comes right to the edge of the track; you see no animal life, or rather you rarely see animals and birds. We had travelled for two days and had not seen a kangaroo. Oliver Ford began to doubt their existence. I felt I had let him down badly in this matter, for I had told him that the whole place was stuffed with kangaroos; then a group of emus crossed the track and on an impulse I turned off into the bush after them. We chased these emus for a few minutes and could not find them. Returning to the track we could not find that either. Oliver Ford was the tallest among us by some measure so he climbed on top of the vehicle, but he could see nothing, just bush. The path we had made through the bush, a wise track it had seemed, was now invisible, the saplings back in place, the ground rock hard, no tracks could be found; we were truly lost. We searched and searched and in time we discovered that we were by chance only a few yards from what passed for our road.

When I remember Oliver Ford it is not fine curtains and grand houses I think of, but the Tanami track, the banks of the Diamantina river and the Simpson desert, sleeping on the sand in a swag under the stars, more stars than in all heavens put together. He was to my wife Romilly and I a good friend.

CONCLUSION

ONCE again I have disposed of 'a collection', or rather the stock of my antique shop. The market at the moment is not favourable for dealing in antiques and I intended to reduce the scale of my operations to suit that market. With a few exceptions, all my stock sold and to my great delight Sotheby's had over 450 clients bid in the sale. I am pleased that old bones and curious stones appeal to people other than myself. Had no one cared for natural curiosities it would not have stopped me from buying them in the first place, for I have never been a collector who followed fashions or, for that matter, a collector who made fashion. I have bought works of art – both natural and man-made – that appealed to me. I have bought objects for no better reason than that I thought their shape to be beautiful, or paintings for their colour and composition.

I have taken as much pleasure from watching the sun go down over the northern coast of Western Australia, where it seemed for a moment or two that all the world was on fire, as I have from the painting by George Stubbs of the Baron De Roebuck on his rearing horse with his galloping dog at his side. I have woken and, in the early morning light, looked at that painting, which once hung on the wall opposite the bottom of my bed, seeing not the work of Stubbs but the influence of Giorgione.

Apart from the convenience of having a particular work in my house, I care not a jot for ownership. I am a nomad, both in my taste and in my habit, drawing what I will from a painting or a place and then moving on. Never feeling the distress of departure, only the excitement of arrival; not restless, but blessed, or cursed, with incurable curiosity.